PREPARE

OUR WORLD IS CHANGING. SIMPLE AND EASY
WAYS FOR URBAN RESIDENTS TO BE READY.

TRAVIS L. CRYAN

TLC_TRNG

CONTENTS

INTRODUCTION

It was a hot August afternoon, and I was going door to door in an apartment building in Southeast Washington, D.C., checking on the residents. The building had been without air conditioning for several days, and now the water was also out in the area. The residents ranged from young to old, healthy to medically fragile. Not having air conditioning for several days was not good for any of them, but losing running water on top of that could be life-threatening. This confluence of events was something none of them were prepared for. No fan to plug into the wall. No case of bottled water to get them started until more could be delivered. This moment stuck with me. It showed how a little foresight could have changed everything.

Urban living complicates disaster preparedness. Cities are complex and unpredictable, brimming with challenges. Many of us feel overwhelmed by the idea of preparing for crises. The hustle and bustle of urban life leave little room for thoughts of emergencies. Space is limited, time is precious, and let's face it, the thought of becoming a "prepper" feels extreme. But what if there was a way to prepare that fit your lifestyle without turning your apartment into a bunker?

That's where this book comes in. Urban residents need a guide tailored to their unique environment. Many resources overlook the intricacies of city life. They miss the mark on providing actionable, simple steps that fit into our daily routines. This book aims to fill that gap. It's about making preparedness approachable, even in the heart of a city.

The core purpose of this book is empowerment. I want to give you practical, manageable steps to get ready for disasters. You don't need to feel like a doomsday prepper to be prepared. It's about building resilience and self-reliance. This isn't just about surviving; it's about thriving in uncertain times.

If you're an adult living in an urban area, this book is for you. You might be concerned about space, money, or just where to start. You're not alone. Many city dwellers share these concerns. This book will address them head-on, offering solutions that fit into your life, not disrupt it.

I bring over 25 years of experience in emergency management to these pages. I've been on the front lines, from flood zones to civil unrest in our nation's capital. My journey began as an EMT and then as a Paramedic in a small community in Western North Carolina that faced many of its own unique challenges from incidents and disasters. Over the years, I've spent countless hours trying to help prepare our infrastructure and governments for worst-case scenarios to help limit the impact on you, the individual, or the family that depends on the world around them to work correctly. Unfortunately, nothing can ever be entirely prevented or prepared for. I've seen firsthand how individual preparedness impacts community outcomes. Those that prepared, even just a little, had much better outcomes than those that did not. Those outcomes had an exponential impact on the community's overall resilience.

On top of all of this, I am also an urban dweller who has fully embraced the lifestyle of living high above the street. I'm dependent on the building under me and the city around me. Heck, we even gave up our cars several years ago. However, I have learned how to still be prepared and resilient despite the constraints of apartment and pedestrian living. This experience drives my passion to help others get ready before disaster strikes.

The book is structured to guide you through this process. It includes practical checklists, real-life scenarios, and actionable advice. Each chapter focuses on specific aspects of preparedness, from understanding risks to creating your own emergency plan. You'll find insights that cater to both the seasoned planner and the complete beginner.

I want to inspire a shift in how you view preparedness. It's not about fear, but about taking control and feeling empowered. Common misconceptions paint preparedness as paranoia. This book challenges that notion, promoting community and collective resilience. We are stronger together, and small actions can make a big difference.

Prepare to engage with the content. This isn't a book to read once and shelve. It's a guide to revisit, offering steps that fit seamlessly into urban life. Whether you live in a high-rise or a cozy apartment, these steps are adaptable and practical.

So here's the call to action: take the first step. Preparedness is a journey. It's not a destination you reach and stop. It's about evolving and adapting. Join me in this journey with confidence. Together, we can enhance your resilience and readiness for whatever the future holds.

The time to start is now!

CHAPTER 1

UNDERSTANDING URBAN RISKS

When I first started out in emergency management, I was struck by how little most city dwellers knew about the risks lurking in their own backyards. It was during a routine inspection of a city's flood defenses that I realized the true scope of urban vulnerabilities. The infrastructure was aging, the residents unaware, and the city ill-prepared for even the slightest of disruptions. That day, I met a local woman who had no idea her home was built on a floodplain. Her bewilderment was a stark reminder of the knowledge gap that exists in urban areas. Understanding urban risks is not about predicting every possible disaster but about recognizing the unique challenges your city faces and preparing accordingly.

1.1 MAPPING YOUR CITY'S DISASTER PROFILE

The first step in understanding urban risks is identifying the specific hazards your city encounters. Every urban area has its own set of vulnerabilities, influenced by geography, climate, and infrastructure. Start by reviewing local government resources. Most cities have an emergency management office that provides detailed hazard maps. These maps are gold mines of information, highlighting areas prone to flooding, landslides, or industrial accidents. Historical disaster data can also reveal patterns, such as seasonal flooding or areas prone to wildfires. Understanding these patterns helps you anticipate the kinds of emergencies you might face. Climate change complicates matters further, pushing disaster impacts beyond previously affected areas. For example, areas once safe from flooding may now find themselves at risk due to rising sea levels and increased rainfall.

Next, evaluate your city's infrastructure. Many urban areas ride on the edge of aging systems that can exacerbate disaster impacts. Bridges, roads, and utility networks often bear the brunt of neglect. When disaster strikes, these weak points can lead to significant disruptions. A bridge collapse or a power grid failure can paralyze a city. Consider how supply chain vulnerabilities play into this. Cities rely heavily on external suppliers for food and goods. A single disrupted route can lead to shortages. Subterranean public transportation and utilities, while efficient, are particularly vulnerable to flooding and earthquakes. Understanding these vulnerabilities allows you to plan for contingencies and reduces the impact of unexpected events.

Engaging with community-based risk assessments offers broader insights into urban risks. These assessments involve analyzing hazards, vulnerabilities, and coping strategies within local communities. Attend local community meetings and review publicly available risk assessment reports. Or, if you aren't inclined to participate in the process, you can easily review the currently published risk assessment. Simply google your city + risk assessment or hazard mitigation plan. If you are a data-driven decision-maker, you'll love the treasure trove of historical data.

Reviewing impact stories from urban areas similar to yours can also provide perspective on how different communities handle disasters. Such stories can inspire and inform your preparedness strategies, showcasing just what can fail, how successes can be achieved, and lessons learned from previous experiences with similar situations.

Pro Tip: It's ONLY a lesson learned if you experience something, identify the problem, try to fix it, and then don't run

into the same problem again in the future under similar circumstances.

Technology plays a crucial role in gathering and analyzing data about urban risks. Use weather forecasting and alert apps to stay informed about impending threats. These apps provide real-time updates, ensuring you're not caught off guard. Neighborhood communication apps can connect you with others in your area, facilitating information sharing and coordination during emergencies. Disaster alert apps offer notifications and advice specific to your location, helping you respond quickly and effectively. Many cities also use Geographic Information Systems (GIS), or mapping software, as another powerful tool. This allows you to visualize and analyze spatial data about your city's vulnerabilities. You can usually find them on your city's urban planning website, and often, your local emergency management website will redirect you to them. These technological resources empower you to make informed decisions, enhancing your readiness for potential disasters.

Another way to understand this information is to watch your local news. I'm not talking about the doom and gloom of the national news, although it has a place in understanding the world. Your local news will have its finger on the pulse of the community you live in and how events like the weather are impacting it. Watch for trends, not just one-off instances.

Pro Tip: *If you are hearing the word "unprecedented," that is your cue to pay attention. While it may seem overused, that just means that the world around us is changing too quickly for us to keep up.*

1.2 UNDERSTANDING WHY URBAN THREATS MATTER

When considering urban threats, the focus shouldn't solely rest on the causes, but rather on the impacts these threats have on daily life. A power outage, for instance, might stem from a natural disaster or a technical glitch, but the result is the same—dark buildings, non-functioning appliances, and a pause in productivity. These impacts, rather than the events that trigger them, are what disrupts our lives. They strip away the conveniences we take for granted. Imagine losing access to clean water, or suddenly finding that grocery store shelves are bare. These scenarios illustrate how different threats can converge into a single, challenging reality.

Power outages stand as one of the most common threats in urban areas. Cities thrive on electricity, so when the grid fails, chaos often follows. Without power, elevators halt, communication networks falter, and food spoilage becomes a real concern. Urban flooding is another high-probability event that disrupts city life. Streets transform into rivers, making transportation unsafe and damaging property. If you live in a seismic zone, earthquakes pose a constant threat. The ground may shake without warning, causing structural damage and endangering lives. Preparing for these events involves more than just stocking up on supplies; it's about understanding how each can uniquely impact your environment and taking steps to mitigate those effects.

Urbanization brings with it an increased risk of man-made disasters. Industrial accidents can release hazardous materials, posing immediate threats to health and safety. City infrastructures are also vulnerable to cyber-attacks, which can cripple essential services like water and electricity or even hospitals and telecommunications. Political unrest can escalate into civil disorder, affecting daily commutes and creating safety concerns. Terrorism, though less frequent, remains a potential threat that can have devastating impacts.

Due to dense populations, public health risks in urban settings can escalate quickly. Disease outbreaks, whether influenza or something more sinister, spread rapidly in cities. Air quality issues, exacerbated by pollution and industrial activity, impact respiratory health, especially in vulnerable populations. These health risks are amplified in urban areas, where close living quarters and shared public spaces facilitate faster transmission. Understanding these risks allows you to prioritize health-related preparedness measures, such as having a supply of masks and maintaining up-to-date vaccinations.

Each of these scenarios requires a specific preparedness strategy, but ultimately, the basics are the same:

- How are you going to get food and water?
- How are you getting the assistance you need? (medical, transportation, financial, etc)
- How long can you get by without electricity?
- How are you staying informed about local emergency and security updates?

To navigate these threats effectively, integrating local knowledge becomes invaluable. Information from local emergency managers can provide insights into city-specific risks and preparedness initiatives. Collaboration with non-governmental organizations (NGOs) offers access to community-focused strategies and resources. These organizations often work on the ground, addressing issues like food security and public health. Their expertise and resources can enhance your understanding of local threats and inform your preparedness efforts.

———

Activity: Conduct a Local Risk Assessment

Take an hour to sit down with a map of your city. Mark areas prone to flooding, note hospitals, and locate your nearest emergency services. Use local government websites to gather information on historical disasters and community risk assessments. Jot down any local organizations that focus on disaster preparedness, like the Red Cross, and consider reaching out to learn more about their efforts. This exercise will not only provide a clearer picture of your urban environment but also highlight potential gaps in your preparedness plan.

———

1.3 UNIQUE CHALLENGES OF HIGH-DENSITY LIVING

URBAN LIFE COMES with its own set of unique hurdles, particularly when it comes to preparing for disasters. One of the most pressing challenges is the constraint of space. In high-rise apartments and compact living arrangements, finding storage for emergency supplies is no small feat. Imagine trying to fit a week's worth of food and water in a place where even a broom closet is a luxury. It requires inventive thinking. Utilizing vertical space, like adding shelves above doorways or finding furniture that doubles as storage, can help. Yet, even with clever solutions, space remains a limiting factor. Evacuating from these high-rises poses another problem. Descending dozens of flights of stairs during an emergency isn't just inconvenient; it can be dangerous, especially for those with mobility issues. Elevators often become unusable, leaving many residents in a precarious situation.

The density of urban populations introduces its own set of complications during emergencies. Crowded evacuation routes can become bottlenecks, turning a quick escape into a slow crawl. Think of it as trying to pour gallons of water through a narrow funnel. Emergency services, while robust in cities, can be quickly overwhelmed by sheer numbers. Communication networks suffer the same fate. Too many people trying to connect at once can clog the system, making it hard for vital information to get through. Resources, often plentiful in cities, can become scarce when everyone needs them simultaneously. It's a stark reminder of how abundance can quickly turn into insufficiency when demand spikes. Now, imagine yourself having to be the people deciding who gets those scarce resources first!

Cities thrive on shared resources, but this dependence can become a vulnerability in a crisis. Public transportation is the lifeline for many urban residents. When it falters, as it often does during emergencies, it leaves countless people stranded. Water and food distribution systems, centralized for efficiency, are equally vulnerable. Disrupted supply chains can lead to shortages, leaving shelves bare and taps dry. This reliance on external systems places city dwellers in a precarious position during disasters. When the systems fail, the comforts of city life don't just disappear; they become obstacles to overcome.

Social dynamics in cities add another layer of complexity to disaster preparedness. On one hand, the close proximity can foster community cohesion. People band together, offering help and sharing resources. On the other hand, socio-economic differences can create divides. Those with more resources can fare better, leaving vulnerable populations at greater risk. Cultural differences, too, play a role. Cities are melting pots, filled with diverse communities that may have different approaches to preparedness and crisis management. Understanding these dynamics is crucial for effective disaster response. It's about harnessing the strength of the community while also recognizing and addressing its fractures.

These challenges are not insurmountable, but they require a nuanced approach. It starts with acknowledging the unique constraints of high-density living and understanding how they impact preparedness and response. It involves finding innovative solutions to storage and evacuation issues, recognizing the limitations of public resources, and fostering community resilience. Urban life is a balancing act, especially when it comes to preparing for the unexpected. The key lies in adaptability and understanding the nuances of city living.

Activity: What are Your Challenges?

Take an hour to think through the following:

- What are some ways you could add more storage space to your environment?
- Do you know more than one way to get out of your apartment, the building, your community, and the city?
- What supplies and resources do you have easy access to now that would become hard to get in an emergency, and how long

can you go without them? (What did you have a hard time getting during COVID-19 or the last snowstorm?)

- Who depends on you, and who do you depend on?
- In an emergency, who would you check on you, and who would you check on?

———

1.4 CLIMATE CHANGE AND URBAN VULNERABILITIES

WHILE THIS SECTION is less about your individual preparedness and more about the work of cities and government, it is important to understand that preparedness should be happening at many different levels.

Cities sit at the forefront of climate change impacts, bearing the brunt of rising sea levels and more frequent severe weather events. Coastal cities face an existential threat as sea levels creep upward, gradually swallowing shorelines and eroding the land beneath buildings. It's not just the picturesque beaches at risk; entire communities face displacement. The homes, businesses, and infrastructure that form the backbone of urban life are threatened. Severe weather events are no longer rare occurrences. Hurricanes, intense rainstorms, and heatwaves occur with alarming regularity, testing the resilience of urban areas. These events disrupt daily life, cause significant economic losses, and threaten lives. A sudden storm can flood subways, halt traffic, and leave thousands without power. These disruptions remind us that climate change is not a distant future but a current reality. And one that is only getting worse.

Cities must adopt adaptive strategies to mitigate these climate-related risks. Sustainable building practices are a crucial first step. New constructions should incorporate materials and designs that withstand extreme weather. Consider the role of urban green spaces. These areas not only provide recreational opportunities but also serve as natural flood management systems. Parks and green roofs absorb rainfall, reducing the burden on drainage systems and mitigating flood risks.

Urban planners must prioritize these adaptive measures and ensure cities can withstand the climate's challenges. Retrofitting existing structures is equally important. Strengthening buildings against storms and floods can prevent catastrophic damage. These strategies require investment and commitment but offer significant returns in resilience and safety.

Policy and governance play pivotal roles in addressing climate vulnerabilities. Zoning laws and building codes must evolve to reflect current climate realities. These plans should emphasize disaster risk reduction. Restricting construction in flood-prone areas and mandating resilient designs are practical steps cities can take. Government initiatives should also focus on creating incentives for sustainable practices and encouraging businesses and individuals to adopt eco-friendly measures.

Community engagement is vital in climate adaptation efforts. Local climate action groups can drive meaningful change, rallying residents to advocate for sustainable policies and practices. These groups often lead grassroots initiatives, from tree planting to community solar projects. Participatory planning processes ensure that diverse voices contribute to climate strategies. Residents can share insights and propose solutions during community meetings, fostering a sense of ownership and collective responsibility. Engagement extends beyond local groups to partnerships with NGOs and academic institutions. These collaborations bring expertise and resources, enhancing community efforts to build resilience.

Incorporating climate change into urban planning requires a multifaceted approach. It demands foresight, collaboration, and a willingness to adopt new paradigms. We must view urban vulnerabilities through the lens of climate change, recognizing the interconnectedness of environmental, social, and economic factors. This perspective allows cities to develop strategies that not only address immediate risks but also build long-term resilience. The path forward involves difficult decisions and substantial investments, but the stakes could not be higher.

As urban residents, we have a role to play in shaping the future of our cities on an individual and community level. By advocating for adaptive measures and participating in local initiatives, we can contribute to a more resilient urban landscape. We should do this while ensuring our own personal preparedness. The time to act is now, for ourselves and future generations.

CHAPTER 2

DIGITAL TOOLS FOR URBAN PREPAREDNESS

magine sitting at your favorite café, sipping coffee, when an alert flashes on your phone. It's a warning about a fast-approaching storm. The information is precise and timely, giving you the chance to make a quick decision—head home or stay put and wait it out. This scenario isn't far-fetched. It's the reality made possible by digital tools that keep us connected and informed. In dense urban environments, where chaos can unfold rapidly, having the right apps and alerts on your smartphone can mean the difference between being caught off guard and staying safe. As cities grow and evolve, so do the emergencies that threaten them. This chapter dives into leveraging technology to stay ahead of the curve, ensuring you're always one step ahead.

2.1 ESSENTIAL APPS FOR EMERGENCY ALERTS

In the digital age, your smartphone is more than just a communication device. It's a lifeline, offering access to critical information and alerts that can keep you safe during emergencies. The first step in harnessing this power is understanding the built-in capabilities of your device. All smartphones now come equipped to receive Wireless Emergency Alerts (WEA), a system that sends notifications about severe weather, missing children, and other emergencies. These notifications aren't text messages, and they are actually sent to your device over a separate part of the cellular network. These messages are crafted and initiated by local, state, and federal government officials who then share them with the cellular networks with a request that they be sent to your phone. At present, there is no requirement for the cellular provider to send the message unless the message is issued on behalf. So, if you're sitting in a restaurant and someone else's phone goes off and yours doesn't, you probably have different providers.

A common example of this kind of notification are the AMBER Alerts and National Weather Service warnings that pop up on your lock screen. A well-crafted message, like those from the NWS, will follow a research-based format established in the Warning Lexicon (2024). They should use as many of the 360 characters allowed for these notifications to tell you:

Who the SENDER is.

What the HAZARD is.

How it will IMPACT you.

The LOCATION of the hazard or where you can find safety.

The PROTECTIVE ACTIONS you should take to help yourself.

The TIME the hazard will start, be over, or when you should take action by.

Where you can go to get additional information.

These messages should also use words that everyone can understand and only use CAPS sparingly to get your attention. If your local public safety agencies don't seem to be following this format, this is a great place to engage with them and encourage them to take the free Effective Message Design training supported by FEMA.

(Yes, that was a shameless plug for a class I helped develop and deliver!)

If you receive too many of these alerts, you've probably been tempted to adjust your notification settings or may already have. I'll be one of the first to tell you that the AMBER Alert notifications are problematic right now, but I also know the people trying to fix them. If you have turned those off, we understand. However, we **HIGHLY** encourage you to keep the other emergency and public safety alerts ON.

Beyond the built-in alerts, it's wise to download additional apps that cater to specific emergencies in your area. Local news and weather apps provide real-time updates on conditions affecting your city. By signing up for local notification services, you tap into a wealth of localized information, from community announcements to neighborhood safety alerts. You can usually find these through your local emergency management or police website. These services keep you connected to your community and informed about events that might impact your daily life. Apps like the FEMA App offer resources and alerts tailored to your location, ensuring you have the latest information at your fingertips. Noonlight, as recommended by Wired, stands out as a top safety app, offering features like emergency alerts and GPS tracking, making it a valuable addition to your digital toolkit. PulsePoint is another great app that lets you know what is happening around you, including when someone nearby needs CPR and where the nearest AED is located.

Customizing your app settings is crucial for maximizing their utility. Set location-based alerts to ensure you receive notifications relevant to your immediate area. This feature is particularly useful if you live in a large city where conditions can vary significantly from one neighborhood to another. Additionally, adjust your notification preferences to focus on specific threats, whether they be weather-related or security concerns. This targeted approach prevents information overload and ensures you receive alerts pertinent to your safety and well-being.

Integrating these apps into your daily routine ensures you're always prepared. For example, you can make checking alerts part of your commute, giving you foresight about potential disruptions or hazards. Many apps sync seamlessly with smart home devices, enhancing your awareness even when you're at home. Imagine receiving a notification on your phone that triggers a smart speaker announcement, alerting everyone in your household about an impending storm. It's a simple yet effective way to keep everyone informed and safe.

When selecting alert apps, it's essential to evaluate their credibility. Start by reviewing app ratings and user feedback, which offer insights into their reliability and effectiveness. Look for apps with official endorsements or partnerships from recognized authorities, as these often indicate a higher level of trustworthiness. A credible app not only provides accurate information but does so in a timely manner, ensuring you're always a step ahead of potential threats.

Activity: Your Alert and Settings

Take a moment to explore the settings on your smartphone. Make sure your Wireless Emergency Alerts are turned ON to ensure you receive the most emergent notifications. Find your local opt-in notification system and sign up for the types of alerts that are most important to you, whether they're related to weather, safety, or community events. Download a local news app and enable location-based alerts. This exercise will help you streamline your alerts, making them an integral part of your preparedness strategy.

INCORPORATING these digital tools into your preparedness plan transforms your smartphone into a powerful ally. With the right apps and alerts, you're equipped to face the unpredictability of urban life head-on, confident in your ability to navigate emergencies with poise and precision.

2.2 USING TECHNOLOGY FOR REAL-TIME UPDATES

In the digital realm of urban living, social media platforms have emerged as indispensable tools during emergencies. Imagine scrolling through X (Formerly Twitter) or Bluesky Social, where a hashtag suddenly trends, alerting you to a fire in a nearby neighborhood. By following official emergency management and public safety accounts, you stay connected to timely updates straight from the source. These accounts often provide critical information faster than traditional media. However, the vastness of social media also means it's a breeding ground for misinformation. It's crucial to hone your skills in distinguishing fact from fiction. Look for verified accounts and cross-check information with official announcements. Remember, amid an emergency, clarity is your best ally.

While social media is a vital tool, it should be complemented with information from government and news websites and accounts. These platforms serve as the backbone of reliable updates. The National Weather Service, for instance, offers precise weather forecasts and alerts, crucial for those living in areas prone to sudden climatic changes. Local news websites and accounts provide area-specific information detailing road closures, evacuation orders, and community resources. These sources often have dedicated sections for emergency news, ensuring you don't miss out on critical developments affecting your area. By bookmarking these websites on your devices, you create a quick-access portal to essential information. Always prioritize official sources to ensure the accuracy of the details you're acting upon.

In the age of digital connectivity, crowdsourced information offers a unique perspective, often filling gaps left by official channels. Apps like Waze leverage community input to provide real-time traffic conditions. Imagine navigating through a city where every road seems blocked, and Waze guides you through less congested routes, thanks to insights from fellow commuters. Reddit communities also serve as a valuable resource. Local subreddits often feature eyewitness reports, offering on-the-ground perspectives that might not immediately reach mainstream media. While these platforms can provide rapid updates, it's important to approach them with a critical eye, verifying information before relying on it for decision-making.

Live streaming services revolutionize how we access news, offering unfiltered glimpses into unfolding events. Platforms like YouTube host live news channels, delivering real-time coverage without the edits and delays of traditional broadcasts. Tuning into these streams during an emergency ensures you're receiving the latest developments as they happen. Additionally, official press conferences are often streamed online, providing direct communication from authorities. These streams allow you to hear crucial information firsthand, free from media interpretation or bias. By subscribing to channels of reputable news organizations and government agencies, you ensure you have a direct line to vital updates when it matters most.

Case Study: Social Media in Emergency Response

During Hurricane Sandy in October 2012, social media played a pivotal role in disseminating information. Residents used Twitter to report downed power lines and flooded streets, while officials utilized the platform to issue real-time evacuation orders. Platforms like Facebook and Instagram became hubs for community support, with users organizing relief efforts and sharing resources. Twelve years later, in the aftermath of Hurricane Helene's devastating impacts on Western North Carolina, social media became a hotbed of politicized misinformation that threatened many parts of the response. These cases highlight the power of social media in emergencies, but it also underscores the need for vigilance in verifying information amidst the chaos.

BY WEAVING these digital tools into your preparedness plan, you create a robust network of information sources. Each platform plays a unique role, from the immediacy of social media to the depth of government websites. Together, they form a comprehensive system, ensuring you remain informed and ready to act, no matter what urban life throws your way.

2.3 DIGITAL COMMUNICATION STRATEGIES DURING DISASTERS

In the heart of a bustling city, communication is your lifeline during a crisis. The first step is crafting a multichannel communication plan that ensures you're always connected, no matter the circumstances. Think of it as having multiple roads leading to the same destination, so even if one path is blocked, you still have options. SMS and messaging apps are your go-to for quick updates. They're efficient, reliable, and can reach people even when networks are strained. Complement these with email alerts for detailed information, which is especially important when you need to convey complex instructions or updates. Email might not be as immediate as a text, but it provides a platform for sharing extensive information, which can be crucial when coordinating plans or updates with a larger group.

Group messaging features are invaluable for keeping everyone on the same page. Imagine the peace of mind you get from knowing your family and friends are just a tap away. Apps like WhatsApp allow you to set up family alert groups, where everyone can communicate in real time, sharing their status and any relevant updates. For broader community coordination, platforms like Slack offer channels where community members can discuss strategies, share resources, and offer support. These tools are particularly useful in densely populated urban areas, where reaching out individually can become cumbersome and time-consuming. By setting up dedicated groups, you ensure that everyone involved has access to the same information, reducing confusion and facilitating a coordinated response.

Communication redundancy is not just a luxury; it's a necessity. Imagine relying solely on your smartphone, only to find the network down when you need it most. That's where backup methods come into play. Traditional walkie-talkies that are available from the outdoor section of many stores or online work great for short-range or line-of-sight communications with people in your area. Walkie-talkie apps can also serve as excellent alternatives, operating over Wi-Fi or offline if needed, providing a direct line to those in your vicinity. For those in remote areas or when traditional networks fail, satellite communication devices offer a robust and reliable solution. They don't rely on cell towers, making them particularly useful in widespread outages or areas with poor reception. In fact, if you have an iPhone with iOS 18 or later, you should familiarize yourself with how to connect it to a satellite in an emergency so that you can use the features for Emergency SOS, texting, and location sharing. Having these alternatives ensures you're never left in the dark, maintaining a vital link to your network.

Practicing digital communication strategies is akin to rehearsing a fire drill. Regular practice ensures everyone knows their role and can act swiftly when required. Schedule group check-ins via your chosen apps, creating a routine that becomes second nature. These check-ins are not just about verifying that lines of communication work; they also reinforce the habit of staying connected. Similarly, test your emergency contact lists for accuracy. Update them regularly to account for any changes in numbers or new additions. This diligence ensures that in the heat of a crisis, reaching out is seamless and stress-free, allowing you to focus on what truly matters—safety and coordination.

In the urban landscape, where the unexpected can happen at any moment, a robust communication plan is your anchor. It's about being prepared, staying connected, and ensuring that you have the means to reach out and stay informed no matter what. This preparation isn't just about technology; it's about building a support network that can weather any storm and keep you safe and informed.

Stories from the impacts of Hurricane Helene on the mountains of Western North Carolina really drive this point home. Not only did the area lose cellular service, but in many areas power and internet were out as well. Radio and word of mouth became the only forms of communication with each other and the outside world for days and weeks. This absence of the real-time communication we have come to depend on also helped drive the rampant mis- and disinformation that surrounded the initial response efforts.

2.4 MAPPING YOUR CITY WITH TECH TOOLS

In the urban jungle, knowing your way around isn't just about getting from point A to B; it's about survival. Mapping apps like Google Maps and Apple Maps have become indispensable tools for planning evacuation routes and identifying safe zones. Imagine a sudden evacuation order due to an approaching hurricane. With a few taps on your phone, you can chart the quickest route to safety, avoiding congested areas that could slow you down. These apps provide real-time traffic updates, allowing you to navigate around obstacles and reach your destination swiftly. Familiarize yourself with these digital maps before any crisis strikes. Spend some time exploring different routes to your workplace, local emergency shelters, or family meeting points. This readiness gives you a mental map of your city, making it easier to adapt when every second counts.

Beyond evacuation routes, mapping apps can help you pinpoint key locations, which are crucial during emergencies. Hospitals, emergency shelters, supply stores, and gas stations are vital lifelines that should be marked on your digital map. The ability to locate these services quickly can be the difference between a minor inconvenience and a major disaster. For instance, if a power outage leaves you without fuel, knowing the nearest gas or charging station can save you time and stress. As part of your preparedness plan, create a custom map highlighting these essential spots. This personalized map becomes a quick reference guide, streamlining your response when the unexpected occurs. It's not just about having the right tools but using them effectively to ensure you're never caught off guard.

Creating custom maps for your family is another strategic move. These maps can include designated meeting points, alternate routes, and safe havens. Imagine a scenario where a family member gets separated during an evacuation. Having a pre-marked meeting spot on your map ensures everyone knows where to regroup. Highlighting alternate routes offers flexibility, allowing you to adapt if your primary route becomes impassable. These personalized maps act as your family's blueprint for safety, providing peace of mind that everyone knows the plan and can execute it even under pressure. Encourage each family member to familiarize themselves with these maps, turning them into a shared resource that enhances collective preparedness.

Satellite imagery offers another layer of situational awareness, giving you a bird's-eye view of your surroundings. By using satellite views, you gain a clearer understanding of the geography, spotting potential hazard areas and identifying safe spaces. This perspective enhances your spatial awareness, helping you gauge distances between landmarks and plan accordingly. For instance, knowing how far a floodplain extends or which areas are prone to landslides can inform your evacuation plans and preparedness strategies. Regularly reviewing satellite imagery familiarizes you with the lay of the land, ensuring you're always one step ahead.

Maps are more than just tools for navigation; they're your guide to understanding and mastering your urban environment. By integrating these digital resources into your preparedness efforts, you create a comprehensive network of information that empowers you to act decisively and confidently. From planning escape routes to identifying essential services, technology transforms how you prepare for and respond to emergencies. These tools offer the foresight needed to anticipate challenges and the flexibility to adapt as situations evolve. As you harness the power of mapping technology, remember that the key lies in preparation and practice. The more familiar you are with these digital tools, the more effectively you'll use them when it matters most.

In today's urban landscape, where change is constant and surprises are inevitable, digital mapping tools are your allies. They offer a unique blend of practicality and innovation, providing the insights and information needed to navigate the complexities of city life. As you continue using these tools, you'll find confidence in your ability to respond to emergencies with clarity and composure. This chapter's insights set the stage for further exploration into urban preparedness strategies. Armed with this knowledge, you're ready to delve deeper into creating a robust plan that encompasses all aspects of urban living. Next, we'll explore how to build an affordable emergency kit tailored to the unique demands of your environment.

CHAPTER 3
BUILDING AN AFFORDABLE EMERGENCY KIT

Imagine standing in your kitchen after a long day, ready to unwind, when suddenly the power goes out. It's pitch black. You fumble for your phone's flashlight and realize you have no idea where the candles are. This is the kind of scenario that makes you think about preparedness. Yet, the idea of building an emergency kit often feels overwhelming, especially on a budget. But let me assure you, it doesn't have to be. You can put together an effective emergency kit without breaking the bank. It's about prioritizing essentials and making smart choices with the resources you have.

3.1 ESSENTIAL ITEMS ON A SHOESTRING BUDGET

When you're building an emergency kit, the first step is to focus on the essentials. Think of it as creating a foundation for survival. Start with non-perishable foods that have a long shelf life. Dry cereals, canned goods, and peanut butter are excellent choices. Not only do they last, but they also provide the necessary nutrients to keep you going when access to fresh food is limited. Water is another critical component. Aim for at least a two-week supply, stored in bleach-purified bottles if possible. If storage space is tight, consider water purification tablets as a compact alternative. Basic sanitary supplies, like soap, hand sanitizer, and toilet paper, ensure you maintain hygiene even when conditions are less than ideal. These core items form the backbone of your kit, addressing immediate survival needs.

Finding inexpensive alternatives can significantly reduce the cost of your emergency kit. Generic brands often offer the same quality as name brands at a fraction of the price. When it comes to tools, opt for multi-use gadgets instead of single-purpose ones. A Swiss Army knife, for example, provides multiple functions in one compact tool. This approach saves space and money, making it easier to manage your kit. Look for deals at dollar stores and discount retailers, where you can find many essentials at lower prices. Remember, the goal is to ensure accessibility for all budgets, making preparedness attainable for everyone.

Buying in bulk is another effective strategy for saving money. Warehouse clubs offer bulk non-perishables at a lower cost per unit, allowing you to stock up without overspending. Consider teaming up with friends or community members for group buying. This way, you can split the cost and share resources, making bulk purchases more affordable. Not only does this approach stretch your dollar further, but it also fosters a sense of community and collaboration. When everyone pitches in, preparedness becomes a shared responsibility, lightening the load for all involved.

Strategic sales and discounts can also help you build your kit without breaking the bank. End-of-season sales are a goldmine for discounted items, from camping gear to non-perishable foods. Coupons and promotional offers further reduce costs, allowing you to stock up on essentials at a fraction of the usual price. Planning ahead is key. By gradually building your kit over time, you can take advantage of sales and avoid the pitfalls of price gouging during emergencies. This proactive approach ensures you're prepared when it matters most without straining your finances.

Activity: Rotation Calendar

Create a rotation calendar for your emergency supplies. List the items you have, and set reminders to check them for freshness and damage. This practice ensures your supplies remain in top condition and ready for use at any moment. For bottled water, check the expiration date and replace it as needed to ensure safety. Canned goods should be inspected for dents or rust, and rotated out accordingly. By keeping your supplies fresh, you maintain the integrity of your emergency kit, ensuring it's reliable when you need it most. This also helps you remember what you have and ensures that you aren't stuck eating something you don't like when you're already distressed by the emergency.

IN THE WORLD of urban preparedness, building an emergency kit on a budget is not only possible—it's practical. By focusing on essentials, exploring cost-effective alternatives, and taking advantage of sales and bulk buying, you can create a comprehensive kit that meets your needs without emptying your wallet. This chapter's strategies empower you to approach preparedness with confidence, knowing you've laid the groundwork for resilience and readiness.

3.2 DIY FIRST-AID KITS FOR URBANITES

Picture yourself on a bustling city street when someone suddenly trips and falls. You reach for your first-aid kit, neatly tucked in your bag, ready to assist. This scenario highlights the importance of having a well-prepared first-aid kit, especially in urban settings where accidents can happen at any moment. Building a first-aid kit tailored for city life involves focusing on the essentials. Start with disposable gloves for your protection and then a variety of bandages and antiseptic wipes. These are your frontline defense against cuts and scrapes. Stock up on prescription medications, ensuring you have enough to last during emergencies when pharmacies might be inaccessible. Many pharmacies can help you work with your doctor to make this easier, especially for life-saving medications. Consider including over-the-counter pain relievers and allergy medications, as they address common ailments quickly and efficiently. These basic components ensure you're equipped to handle minor injuries and conditions, providing peace of mind as you navigate the city.

Creating some first-aid items at home saves money and adds a personal touch to your kit. For instance, you can make DIY antiseptic solutions using common household items like vinegar and water, which can effectively clean wounds. Homemade cold compresses are another useful addition. Fill a ziplock bag with ice or frozen peas, wrapping it in a cloth for a simple yet effective remedy for swelling or bruises. These homemade alternatives are cost-effective, easy to prepare, and ensure you're never caught off guard when minor injuries arise. They also allow you to customize your kit to suit your needs, making it uniquely yours.

In the realm of first-aid supplies, versatility is key. Opt for items that can serve multiple purposes, reducing the need for numerous single-use products. Cloth bandages, for instance, can be washed and reused, providing a sustainable alternative to disposable ones. Scissors and tweezers are invaluable tools, not just for cutting bandages but for a variety of tasks, from opening packaging to removing splinters. Their multi-use potential makes them indispensable in any first-aid kit, ensuring you're prepared for a range of situations. By focusing on reusable and versatile items, you create a kit that's both efficient and environmentally friendly, aligning with the growing trend of sustainability in urban living.

Crafting a compact and portable first-aid kit is essential for urbanites, who often find themselves on the move. Choose containers that are easy to carry, like small pouches or compact boxes. These can be slipped into a backpack or handbag without taking up much space. Organize your supplies using ziplock bags, grouping similar items together for easy access. This method of organization prevents fumbling during emergencies, allowing you to quickly find what you need. A well-organized kit ensures that you're ready to respond promptly, whether you're at work, commuting, or enjoying a day out in the city. The convenience of a portable kit cannot be overstated, as it allows you to keep essential supplies within reach at all times.

Activity: Create a List of First-Aid Kit Essentials

Compile a list of essential first-aid items for your kit, including bandages, antiseptic wipes, prescription medications, pain relievers, and allergy medication. Add homemade solutions like DIY antiseptics and cold compresses. Include multi-use tools such as scissors and tweezers. Store these items in a compact container, organized with ziplock bags for easy access. This resource list serves as a quick reference, ensuring you have all necessary supplies on hand. Also, like your food supply, you should check and rotate these items regularly to make sure they maintain their effectiveness.

INCORPORATING these strategies into your first-aid kit preparation equips you to handle the unexpected confidently. By focusing on essential components, embracing homemade remedies, and prioritizing portability, you create a kit tailored to urban living, providing an invaluable resource for everyday safety.

3.3 REUSING HOUSEHOLD ITEMS FOR PREPAREDNESS

Every urban household has hidden treasures tucked away, items that often go unnoticed but hold great potential in emergency situations. Take that collection of refillable water bottles gathering dust in your kitchen cabinet. They might seem like clutter, but in a pinch, they can be lifesavers. Fill them with water or use them to store other essential liquids. They're durable, portable, and eco-friendly, making them perfect for an emergency kit. Similarly, those plastic containers you keep for leftovers? They can double as storage for small, loose items like matches or batteries, keeping them organized and protected from the elements. In an urban setting where space is a luxury, repurposing these common items can make all the difference in maintaining an effective preparedness strategy.

When it comes to emergency warmth, old blankets are your best friends. They might not be the latest fashion in home decor, but they are invaluable when temperatures drop and heating is unavailable. An old blanket can be used as an extra layer of insulation in a drafty apartment, or as a makeshift barrier against cold air seeping through windows. And don't overlook your everyday pillows. While they might seem like a simple comfort item, in an emergency, they can become makeshift cushions or padding, providing support and protection in unexpected situations. These creative solutions transform ordinary household items into vital components of your emergency plan, proving that preparedness doesn't always require expensive gear or specialized equipment.

Upcycling is an art form that turns waste into something valuable, and it plays a crucial role in emergency preparedness. Consider the clothes you've outgrown or those with minor wear and tear. Instead of discarding them, cut them into strips to create rags or bandages. They're useful for cleaning or as temporary dressings for injuries. Empty jars, often relegated to the recycling bin, can be your secret weapon. They're perfect for waterproof storage, protecting matches, documents, or small electronics from moisture. Upcycling not only reduces waste but also enhances your preparedness by providing practical solutions with items you already own. It's about viewing what you have through a new lens, seeing potential where others might see clutter.

Sustainable practices have found their way into all aspects of life, including emergency preparedness. By reusing items, you reduce waste and lessen your environmental impact, which is increasingly important in urban areas where waste management is a significant concern. Composting organic waste, for example, not only supports your urban garden but also reduces landfill contributions. It's a simple yet effective way to maintain sustainability, even when preparing for the unexpected. Solar-powered devices are another avenue worth exploring. Old electronics, like solar-powered calculators or garden lights, can be repurposed to charge small devices or provide light during power outages. These sustainable practices align with the growing movement towards eco-friendly living, ensuring that your preparedness efforts are responsible and forward-thinking.

Case Study: Urban Preparedness and Creativity

In a recent urban blackout, a family found themselves in the dark with limited resources. They creatively used empty jars to protect their matches and electronics from moisture, ensuring these items remained functional. Old blankets provided warmth, while refillable water bottles stored enough water for several days. This case demonstrates how repurposing everyday items can create an effective emergency plan, showcasing the power of creativity in preparedness.

BY LOOKING AROUND YOUR HOME, you'll discover a wealth of resources that can be repurposed for emergencies. These often overlooked items hold the key to building a comprehensive and cost-effective preparedness plan. It's about thinking outside the box, transforming the mundane into the extraordinary, and realizing that with a little ingenuity, you can turn everyday objects into vital tools for survival. Embrace the potential of what you already have, and you'll find that preparedness is not only achievable but within arm's reach.

3.4 SOURCING AFFORDABLE SUPPLIES LOCALLY

When stepping out into your neighborhood, you might not immediately consider it a treasure trove of emergency supplies, but that's exactly what it can be. Local thrift stores, often overlooked, are goldmines for affordable gear. They stock everything from sturdy backpacks to durable clothing. You might even find camping equipment, such as sleeping bags or portable stoves, at a fraction of retail prices. These items are invaluable when assembling your emergency kit. Farmers' markets, too, offer more than just fresh produce. Many vendors sell bulk food items that can be stored for emergencies, such as grains and dried fruits. Buying in bulk not only fills your pantry but also supports local farmers, creating a win-win situation. By sourcing supplies locally, you tap into a sustainable network that supports both your community and your preparedness efforts.

Community swap meets and sharing initiatives are fantastic for those looking to build their emergency kits without spending a fortune. These gatherings allow you to barter for goods, exchanging items you no longer need for those that can bolster your preparedness. Imagine swapping an extra set of dishes for a portable water filter or trading garden tools for a solar lamp. These exchanges build connections and foster a sense of community, turning preparedness into a collective effort. Community tool libraries are another resource, offering equipment on loan. From power tools to kitchen appliances, these libraries provide access to items you might need in a pinch without the burden of ownership. By participating in these initiatives, you not only save money but also contribute to a culture of sharing and resilience.

Second-hand stores are treasure chests of high-quality, affordable emergency supplies. Stores specializing in camping gear often have a wide array of second-hand products, from tents to lanterns, that are perfect for emergency situations. These stores offer the chance to acquire durable goods without the brand-new price tag. Online marketplaces also provide endless possibilities. Platforms like eBay or Craigslist are filled with listings for used items, including portable generators, flashlights, and emergency radios. With a careful eye and a little patience, you can find excellent deals that make your emergency kit both comprehensive and economical. The key is to remain vigilant and ready to pounce when the right opportunity arises.

Engaging with local organizations can open doors to resources and discounts that make gathering emergency supplies more feasible. Community workshops often offer discounted kits and supplies, providing an affordable way to learn and prepare simultaneously. These workshops can teach you about proper kit assembly, ensuring you know how to use each item effectively. Non-profit organizations also play a pivotal role, especially for those facing financial constraints. Many organizations provide emergency supplies to low-income families, ensuring everyone has access to the resources they need. By connecting with these groups, you gain not only physical supplies but also valuable knowledge and support. This community-oriented approach underscores the importance of working together, both in preparation and during times of crisis.

As you navigate these local avenues, remember that preparedness is a shared responsibility. By leveraging your community's resources, you not only enhance your readiness but also contribute to a resilient network of neighbors ready to support one another. A community's strength lies in its ability to come together, pool resources, and face challenges with unity and determination. The next chapter will explore how to maximize your living space for preparedness, exploring how to store your newfound supplies smartly in even the smallest urban apartments.

CHAPTER 4
SPACE-SMART STORAGE SOLUTIONS

magine standing in your cramped apartment, feeling overwhelmed by the clutter that seems to multiply overnight. It's a familiar scene for many urban dwellers. Space is a precious commodity, and finding room for all your belongings can feel like a never-ending puzzle. But there's a secret weapon at your disposal: vertical storage. By looking upward, you can unlock a wealth of possibilities that transform even the smallest spaces into organized havens. Think of it as turning your walls into storage superheroes, ready to save the day.

The potential of your walls is often underestimated. They're not just barriers between rooms; they're blank canvases waiting to be utilized. Installing wall-mounted shelving units is a game-changer. These units maximize space and keep items like canned goods within reach while freeing up valuable countertop or cabinet space. Imagine walking into your kitchen and seeing rows of neatly organized cans, all thanks to a few well-placed shelves. For those who enjoy a bit of DIY, pegboards offer another layer of organization. They're perfect for hanging tools, utensils, or any small items that tend to get lost in drawers. Not only do they keep things tidy, but they also add a touch of style, turning your walls into functional art.

Moving upwards, let's explore the often-ignored world of overhead storage solutions. Ceiling-mounted racks can bear the burden of bulky items, offering a clever way to clear floor space. These racks are especially useful in homes with high ceilings, where they can serve as both storage and decor, as noted by Homes and Gardens. Picture a bike hanging securely above your head, out of the way yet easily accessible when needed. Hanging baskets, on the other hand, are ideal for lightweight supplies. They dangle gracefully from the ceiling, providing easy access to items like fresh produce or laundry supplies. This approach not only declutters your living area but also infuses a sense of creativity and practicality into your space.

Tall cabinets and bookcases are another essential in the vertical storage arsenal. These towering pieces draw the eye upward, creating the illusion of higher ceilings and more space. Opt for slim, tall cabinets in narrow spaces, where they can tuck neatly against a wall without overpowering the room. Adjustable shelving units add flexibility, allowing you to customize the height of each shelf to suit your storage needs. Whether you're housing books, decorative items, or pantry supplies, tall furniture provides ample storage without consuming precious floor space. It's like having a second closet, only more versatile and aesthetically pleasing.

Organizational tools are key to making the most of your vertical storage. Stackable containers offer a simple yet effective solution for maximizing shelf space. They keep items contained and orderly, making it easy to see what you have at a glance. Implementing a labeling system further enhances accessibility. By clearly marking each container, you eliminate the guesswork and streamline your daily routine. Imagine opening a cabinet and instantly knowing where everything is—no more frantic searches for that elusive can of beans or misplaced pair of scissors. Organizational tools bring a sense of order and efficiency, turning chaos into calm.

————

Activity: Wall Storage Makeover

Take some time to assess your current storage situation. Identify areas where vertical space is underutilized and brainstorm ways to enhance it. Consider adding a shelf or two in your kitchen or installing a pegboard in your workspace. As you make changes, note the improvements in accessibility and organization. This exercise will help you see the potential of your space, inspiring further innovations in your storage strategy.

————

BY EMBRACING VERTICAL STORAGE, you not only reclaim your living space but also create an environment that reflects your personality and style. It's about finding solutions that work for you and transforming your home into a more functional and enjoyable place to live.

4.2 CREATIVE UNDER-BED STORAGE HACKS

Living in a city often means making the most of every inch of your space. Under-bed storage is one of those underappreciated opportunities that can truly transform your space. It's like having a secret compartment that remains hidden until you need it. Imagine sliding out a low-profile bin filled with non-perishable food, ready and waiting for when you need an extra can of soup or a bag of rice. These bins are perfect for keeping essentials accessible yet out of sight, ensuring your living area stays tidy. They fit snugly under most beds and are designed to maximize storage without adding clutter. Vacuum-sealed bags are another genius solution. They compress clothing and blankets, making them compact and easy to store. Picture a winter comforter that normally takes up an entire closet shelf, now neatly tucked away under the bed, freeing up valuable space for other needs.

Custom-built drawers under your bed can take this storage strategy to the next level. The beauty of custom drawers lies in their ability to fit your specific needs and bed dimensions. If you're handy with tools, installing DIY drawers can be a rewarding project. Imagine crafting a set of drawers that glide effortlessly, revealing neatly organized compartments for shoes, seasonal clothing, or even important documents. For those less inclined toward DIY, ready-made drawer kits offer a convenient alternative. These kits come with everything you need for installation, making the process straightforward. They offer the same benefits without the need for saws and screws. With custom drawers, your bed transforms into a multipurpose unit, providing ample storage without sacrificing style or function.

Bed risers are another clever hack that can significantly increase your under-bed storage capacity. These simple devices lift your bed off the floor, creating extra space beneath. Adjustable bed risers allow you to choose the height that best suits your needs, whether you're storing larger items like suitcases or prefer easy access to everyday essentials. The benefits of this additional space are tremendous. Not only do they provide more room for storage, but they also make cleaning under the bed a breeze. With the extra height, vacuuming or sweeping becomes much easier, helping you maintain a clean and organized living space.

To truly maximize your under-bed storage, consider combining these techniques. Use a mix of low-profile bins for frequently accessed items and vacuum-sealed bags for seasonal storage. Install custom drawers for specialized needs and add bed risers to maximize vertical space. This layered approach ensures you're utilizing every inch available, turning your bed into a powerful storage engine that works discreetly in the background.

Activity: Under-Bed Storage Assessment

Take a moment to inventory the items currently stored under your bed. Are they organized, or is it a jumble of forgotten belongings? Consider what could be stored there more efficiently. Measure the dimensions under your bed and explore options for bins, bags, or drawers that fit. This exercise will help you visualize the potential of your under-bed space, encouraging strategic storage solutions.

————

INCORPORATING under-bed storage solutions into your home frees up space and makes daily living more efficient. It's about transforming hidden nooks into functional storage areas, making your urban living experience more enjoyable and manageable.

4.3 MULTIPURPOSE FURNITURE FOR PREPAREDNESS

In the confines of urban living, where every square foot counts, multipurpose furniture becomes a clever ally. Imagine your living room, a space that morphs seamlessly from day to night, courtesy of a sofa bed with hidden storage. By day, it's a cozy spot for lounging and entertaining guests. By night, it unfolds into a comfortable bed, ready to host overnight visitors. Beneath the cushions, you find storage compartments perfect for extra bedding or seasonal clothes, ensuring you're always prepared without sacrificing style or comfort. Such pieces are not just practical; they offer a sense of luxury that maximizes your living area.

Similarly, tables with built-in compartments provide unexpected storage opportunities. Dining tables often double as workspaces in city apartments, so having a spot to tuck away papers, stationery, or even dining essentials like cutlery and napkins can keep your space tidy. It's about creating environments that are as flexible as your lifestyle demands, adapting to your needs with style and efficiency.

Built-in storage features in furniture allow you to cleverly disguise your preparedness efforts. Ottomans with internal compartments hold blankets, magazines, or emergency supplies, always within reach yet artfully concealed. They serve dual purposes, acting as both a seating area and a storage solution. The key lies in choosing furniture designed to work as hard as you do, offering both functionality and aesthetic appeal. These pieces blend seamlessly with your décor, enhancing your home's style while providing practical benefits.

For those willing to roll up their sleeves, DIY adaptations can further extend your storage capabilities. Existing furniture can be modified to suit your needs, transforming ordinary items into extraordinary storage solutions. Adding shelves to bookcases, for example, increases their capacity, allowing you to organize books, documents, or decorative items neatly. Installing hooks under tables provides a discreet spot for hanging bags, headphones, or kitchen utensils, keeping them off surfaces and out of the way. These simple modifications require minimal effort but offer significant returns, turning everyday furniture into customized storage solutions tailored to your lifestyle.

In the world of urban living, where space is limited and functionality is key, multipurpose furniture offers an elegant solution. It's about finding pieces that serve more than one purpose, allowing your home to adapt to your needs. Whether you're hosting friends, working from home, or storing your preparedness items, these furniture innovations ensure you're always ready without compromising on style or comfort.

CHAPTER 5
PRACTICAL SOLUTIONS FOR POWER OUTAGES

magine a quiet evening in your high-rise apartment, the city lights shimmering like stars against the night sky. Suddenly, the lights flicker and die, plunging your home into an unsettling darkness. In the heart of an urban jungle, this scenario is all too familiar. Power outages, whether from storms or grid failures, can leave you stranded in your own home, especially when you're several stories above ground. Preparing for these blackouts, particularly when living in upper-floor apartments, involves understanding the building systems and how they might be affected.

Familiarizing yourself with your building's power-dependent systems is crucial. Elevators, for instance, are the lifelines in high-rise buildings. When power fails, so do they, potentially trapping residents or making upper floors inaccessible. This makes knowing the location of stairwells and emergency exits not just useful but necessary. Fire safety systems, too, often rely on electricity. While most have backup power, it's essential to know how long these systems can function without the main supply. Emergency lighting might be installed, but understanding its reach and limitations ensures you can navigate safely in the dark. These systems are designed to protect you, but only if you know how to use them. Additionally, the heating and air conditioning systems are also a big drain on a building's power source. So much so that they typically will not work on a backup power source or generator.

Creating an emergency lighting plan tailored for high-rise living can greatly alleviate the stress of a blackout. Battery-operated LED lanterns are excellent for illuminating hallways and common areas, providing consistent light without the fire risk of candles. They're portable, durable, and can easily be moved to where they're needed most. Glow sticks, while often associated with parties, serve as a temporary lighting solution. They're safe, last for hours, and can be placed strategically to mark pathways or stairs. For a more sustainable option, consider solar-powered lights. Placing these near windows during the day ensures they're charged and ready to provide illumination at night. Each of these options offers a simple, effective way to bring light into the darkest of situations, turning your home into a beacon of safety.

Maintaining fresh air and ventilation is another critical aspect, especially when HVAC systems go down. Opening windows is the most straightforward solution, allowing natural ventilation to circulate and refresh the air inside. However, in extreme weather, this might not be feasible. Portable fans, particularly those powered by rechargeable batteries, can be lifesavers. They help maintain airflow without relying on the building's main power. These fans are compact, easy to store, and can make a significant difference in comfort, especially during warmer months. Ensuring you have a few on hand prepares you for those moments when the air feels stifling and a gentle breeze is all you need to feel at ease.

Water supply interruptions present another challenge during blackouts. High-rise buildings often depend on electricity to pump water to upper floors, meaning an outage can disrupt your access. Before any anticipated outage, fill bathtubs and sinks with water. This provides a reserve for flushing toilets and basic sanitation needs. It's a straightforward yet often overlooked step that ensures you're not caught off guard. Additionally, keeping a stock of bottled water is crucial. Aim for at least a gallon per person per day, stored in a cool, dark place. This supply serves as your drinking water, ensuring you stay hydrated even when the taps run dry.

––––––––

Activity: Pre-Outage Checklist

Take a moment to consider what preparations you can make before a power outage hits. Create a checklist that includes filling water containers, charging battery-operated devices, and ensuring all emergency lighting is accessible. Review your building's emergency procedures and familiarize yourself with exit routes. This proactive approach keeps you ready to face any blackout with confidence and clarity.

––––––––

NAVIGATING the challenges of a blackout requires foresight and a little ingenuity. By understanding your building's systems, developing an emergency lighting plan, ensuring fresh air, and planning for water interruptions, you transform potential chaos into manageable scenarios. These steps, while simple, empower you to maintain control and safety in your urban sanctuary, no matter how dark the night becomes.

5.2 PORTABLE POWER OPTIONS FOR APARTMENTS

In the midst of a city blackout, your first thought might be to reach for a backup power source to keep the essentials running. Apartments offer unique challenges when it comes to portable power, so selecting the right equipment is crucial. Portable generators with inverter technology are a great option. They provide a stable power supply that's safe for sensitive electronics, like laptops and phones, which are vital for staying connected and informed. Inverter generators are generally quieter and more efficient than traditional models, making them suitable for apartment living where noise levels are a concern. However, these generators must be used with caution, especially in an urban environment, and ONLY when they can be placed outside for proper ventilation.

A BETTER choice is compact power stations designed specifically for essential electronics. These all-in-one units store power and offer multiple outlets, allowing you to charge devices simultaneously. They are user-friendly and require minimal setup, perfect for those living in smaller spaces. Many of the options are also compatible with solar panels for easy recharging. Solar-powered chargers offer a practical solution, allowing you to keep essential devices like phones and tablets running. According to a review by Outdoor Gear Lab, the BigBlue SolarPowa 28 stands out as one of the best portable solar panels, providing efficient charging capabilities for most devices. These chargers are not just for tech enthusiasts; they're a lifeline in emergencies, ensuring you maintain communication and access to information. Portable solar panels, like the Jackery SolarSaga 100, take it a step further by powering small appliances, which can be a game-changer if the blackout stretches longer than anticipated. Imagine brewing a cup of coffee with solar energy on a chilly morning when the power's out. It's about finding comfort in chaos and using the resources around you to stay resilient.

Exploring alternative power solutions can provide intriguing options for apartment dwellers seeking sustainable and unconventional methods. Pedal-powered generators offer a unique blend of exercise and energy generation. By pedaling, you can charge small electronics like phones or radios, making it a practical solution for those prepared to put in a bit of physical effort. This method is both eco-friendly and an excellent way to stay active during a blackout. Solar window chargers are another innovative choice, especially in sunlit apartments. These chargers harness natural light to power small devices, providing a renewable energy source without the need for extensive equipment. They're compact, easy to use, and perfect for urban settings where space is limited.

Prioritizing which devices to charge during a blackout can make all the difference. Start with mobile phones and communication devices, as these keep you connected with family, friends, and emergency services. Power banks with multiple USB ports are a lifesaver here, enabling you to charge several devices at once. A fully charged phone is more than just a luxury; it's your gateway to information and assistance. Once the essentials are covered, consider charging other important electronics, like laptops or tablets, which can serve as alternate communication tools. Keeping these priorities in mind ensures that you make the most of your limited power resources, maintaining your link to the outside world.

Incorporating these portable power options into your blackout preparedness plan ensures that you remain powered up and ready, no matter how long the lights are out. By selecting the right backup power sources, prioritizing device charging, and exploring alternative options, you equip yourself with the tools to face any outage with confidence. Your apartment becomes a sanctuary of light and connectivity, even when the city around you fades into darkness.

5.3 SAFE COOKING WITHOUT ELECTRICITY

Imagine the power going out just as you're about to start dinner. You're in your kitchen, staring at an electric stove that isn't going to heat a thing. For urban dwellers, losing power doesn't mean losing the ability to cook. There are several safe and effective tools you can use indoors during power outages. Portable gas stoves *(think camp stoves...)*, designed with safety features like automatic shut-offs, are a top choice. They're compact and efficient, allowing you to boil water or heat meals without relying on electricity. Flameless cooking systems and induction plates offer alternative methods. These systems are particularly useful in apartments, where open flames might be a concern. Induction plates use magnetic fields to heat pots directly, providing a flameless solution that's both safe and efficient.

But what if you want to skip cooking altogether? Planning for no-cook meals is a smart strategy. Stock up on pre-packaged, fully cooked, and canned foods, which require no preparation and provide a nutritious option in a pinch. Ready-to-eat meals, often found in camping sections, are another excellent choice. They're designed to be eaten cold or with minimal warming, making them ideal for power outages. Nutrition bars, packed with energy and essentials, are perfect for quick snacks or meals. Keeping these items on hand ensures you're never left without sustenance, even when your kitchen is temporarily out of commission. Having a variety of no-cook options means you can adapt to any situation, maintaining a balanced diet without the hassle of cooking.

When cooking without electricity, safety should always be your priority. If you're using a gas stove, it's crucial to have a carbon monoxide detector installed. This device monitors the air and alerts you if dangerous levels of carbon monoxide are present, ensuring your cooking area remains safe. Keeping a fire extinguisher accessible is another essential precaution. It's one of those items you hope never to use, but it's invaluable if needed. Even the most careful cook can encounter unexpected flare-ups, and having a fire extinguisher nearby provides peace of mind. Adhering to these safety practices helps prevent accidents, allowing you to cook confidently and securely, regardless of the situation.

On a brighter day, consider leveraging outdoor cooking spaces available in your community. Many apartment complexes feature rooftop grills, which offer a fantastic opportunity to cook outdoors while enjoying the cityscape. These communal areas often become social hubs, where neighbors gather and share stories, turning a power outage into a memorable event. Public parks with barbecue facilities are another option, especially during extended outages. They provide a space to cook and connect with others in your community, fostering a sense of resilience and camaraderie. By utilizing these outdoor spaces, you can keep the flames of community spirit alive, even when the power is out.

Cooking without electricity doesn't have to be a challenge. With the right tools, a little planning, and a focus on safety, you can continue enjoying meals and maintaining a sense of normalcy. Whether you choose to cook indoors, rely on no-cook meals, or take advantage of outdoor spaces, remember that adaptability is key. The ability to adjust and find creative solutions ensures that even during a power outage, your kitchen remains the heart of your home.

5.4 MAINTAINING CONNECTIVITY DURING OUTAGES

Power outages can quickly sever our ties to the world, leaving us in a communication void. Yet, maintaining connectivity with family, neighbors, and emergency services is crucial. One effective strategy is the use of battery-powered or manual radios. These devices become your lifeline, providing news updates and emergency broadcasts even when digital networks fail. Unlike smartphones, radios aren't dependent on a charged battery or a working cell tower. Having one on hand ensures you remain informed and receive crucial updates on weather conditions or emergency instructions without interruption. They're reliable and straightforward, cutting through the silence of a blackout with vital information.

Establishing a communication plan with neighbors is another proactive step. In urban settings, where communities are often packed together, neighbors can be invaluable allies. Discussing and setting up a plan before an outage can facilitate information sharing and mutual support. Decide on a meeting point or a system for checking in on each other. This can be as simple as a quick knock on the door or a flashlight signal through the window. By maintaining a line of communication, you foster a sense of community and resilience, ensuring that everyone is aware and accounted for during an emergency. This collective approach turns isolation into connection, building a support network right at your doorstep.

When it comes to accessing information without power, preparation is key. Pre-downloading maps and contact lists onto your devices ensure you have access to crucial information, even when offline. Apps like Google Maps offer offline features that allow you to navigate without an internet connection. Similarly, save important contact numbers and emergency information in a note-taking app, where they can be accessed without Wi-Fi. These small steps ensure that you're not left scrambling for information when the lights go out. They transform your smartphone from a paperweight into a powerful tool, ready to guide you through the uncertainty of a blackout.

Community resources offer another layer of connectivity during outages. Many community centers are equipped with backup power, providing a haven for charging devices and accessing Wi-Fi. These centers often open their doors to residents during emergencies, offering a place to gather, recharge, and share information. Local libraries, too, can serve as internet hubs. While they may not operate 24/7, during their open hours, they provide a valuable resource for staying connected. By utilizing these community assets, you ensure that even when your home is dark, you have a place to find light, both literally and in the form of information and connectivity.

For extended outages, long-term strategies become essential. Investing in long-range walkie-talkies or getting your ham radio license can be a way to maintain communication over distances, providing a reliable way to stay in touch with family or neighbors, even when cellular networks are down. These devices don't rely on external infrastructure, making them particularly useful in prolonged blackouts. Setting up a neighborhood information board is another effective method. This board can serve as a central point for sharing updates, resources, and messages. It's a low-tech solution that fosters community spirit, ensuring everyone remains informed and connected, no matter how long the outage lasts.

As we navigate the challenges of urban living, maintaining connectivity during power outages becomes a vital skill. By combining traditional methods like radios with modern technology and community resources, you create a robust network that keeps you informed and connected. This chapter's insights equip you with practical tools and strategies to ensure that even when the power is out, you're never left in the dark. As we continue, let's explore how urban preparedness extends beyond immediate crises, focusing on long-term sustainability and resilience.

MAKE a Difference with Your Review

Unlock the Power of Generosity

"Helping one person might not change the world, but it could change the world for one person." – Anonymous

Preparedness is about community. It's about looking out for each other, even in the smallest ways. And today, you can make a big impact with just a few words. ***Would you help someone just like you—interested in disaster preparedness but feeling unsure about where to begin?***

My mission with ***PREPARE*** is simple: to make preparing for emergencies approachable and practical for everyone. Whether you're new to the idea or have been meaning to start, this book will guide you step by step.

But to reach more people who need this guidance, I need your help.

Most people pick up books because of reviews. That's why I'm asking you to share your thoughts about *PREPARE*.
It won't cost you a thing, and it only takes a minute. But your review could:

- Help a family feel confident in their ability to face the unexpected.
- Encourage a busy parent to start preparing without feeling overwhelmed.
- Inspire someone in a small apartment to take their first step toward readiness.

To make a difference, simply scan the QR code or visit the link below to leave your review:

Click Here to Review this book on Amazon

If you care about building stronger, more prepared communities, you're exactly the kind of person this book was written for. Thank you from the bottom of my heart for helping spread this important message!

Travis L. Cryan

CHAPTER 6
EVACUATION PLANNING IN URBAN AREAS

The city hums with life, a tapestry of lights and sounds. You're sitting in your favorite coffee shop, savoring a moment of quiet amid the urban bustle. Suddenly, your phone buzzes with an alert. An emergency evacuation order flashes across the screen. The thought of navigating the city in a crisis can be daunting, especially when everyone seems to have the same idea—hit the road. But what if you didn't have to rely solely on your car? Could the very transit systems you use daily become your allies in an emergency? Picture this: instead of fighting gridlock, you glide through the city on a bus or subway, part of a well-crafted public transit evacuation plan that gets you and others to safety efficiently.

Crafting a public transit evacuation plan begins with understanding your city's transit options. In many urban areas, subway systems serve as the arteries of the city. Their operational hours, however, can vary. During an emergency, knowing whether the subway will be running and which lines might be operational is crucial. If your city has a network of buses assess which routes cover key evacuation areas. Some buses might be rerouted or repurposed to ferry evacuees to safety, making them a valuable resource. The key is to familiarize yourself with these routes and understand their limitations during crises. For example, a study highlighted on ResearchGate emphasizes optimizing bus capacity and identifying effective evacuation routes and pickup points, which can be critical during no-notice evacuations.

Developing a flexible evacuation strategy is essential, as public transit systems can be unpredictable during emergencies. Create multiple alternate routes, considering various forms of transportation. If the subway is down, buses might still offer a viable escape route. But what if both are offline? Rideshares or taxis can provide backup options, though availability might be limited. Uber and Lyft both have programs in place to coordinate with local emergency managers to provide evacuation support. However, the availability and capacity are dependent on driver availability. Remember, most rideshare drivers are using their own vehicles and have their own families to worry about. Flexibility is your friend. The more options you have, the better prepared you'll be to adapt to changing conditions. Think of your evacuation strategy as a puzzle. The pieces might shift, but with careful planning, they'll fit together when it matters most.

Researching plans posted by local transit authorities is another vital step in ensuring your evacuation plan is effective. Many cities have official transit communication channels, such as apps or websites, that provide real-time updates during emergencies. Subscribing to these channels ensures you're informed about any changes to routes or services. Public meetings with transit officials can also offer valuable insights. These forums provide a platform for discussing concerns, learning about contingency plans, and understanding how the transit system will operate during a crisis. By staying informed and engaged, you become an active participant in your safety rather than a passive observer.

Preparing for non-standard transit situations is crucial, as emergencies can transform the usual commute into a chaotic endeavor. Crowded or limited-capacity vehicles are often the norm, so having a plan for navigating these conditions is key. Knowing which transit stations might serve as temporary shelters can also be beneficial. These locations often become hubs for information and resources, offering a place to regroup and reassess your next steps. In some cases, transit stations may provide basic amenities or connect you with emergency services, turning them into valuable assets during evacuation. By preparing for these non-standard situations, you enhance your ability to remain calm and decisive under pressure.

———

Case Study: Urban Transit in Crisis

During a sudden flash flood, the city's transit system became a lifeline for thousands. Buses were repurposed to shuttle evacuees to higher ground. Subway stations, which typically served as temporary shelters, providing refuge and resources, had to be closed due to flooding. High-rise buildings near the closed subway stations, with ample open space on the second floor and above, had to quickly be identified as shelters of last resort. This case demonstrates the importance of understanding and leveraging public transit during emergencies, turning a potential liability into a strategic advantage.

———

IN THE URBAN LANDSCAPE, where density and complexity reign, crafting a personal evacuation plan that includes public transit can be a game-changer. By assessing your options, developing a flexible strategy, coordinating with authorities, and preparing for unusual conditions, you transform the chaos of an emergency into an organized and efficient escape.

6.2 IDENTIFYING CITY-SPECIFIC EVACUATION ROUTES

Understanding your city's evacuation routes is like having an essential map to safety tucked in your back pocket. You may think of your city as a sprawling web of streets and avenues, but within this complexity lie designated paths designed to guide you out during emergencies. These official evacuation routes have been mapped out by city planning departments and are crucial for your preparedness plan. Getting your hands on these maps is easier than you might think. Many city websites offer downloadable versions, while others provide hard copies at local government offices. Along with maps, keep an eye out for signposted routes within the city. These signs can be lifesavers, especially in the chaos of a hurried evacuation where every second counts.

Geography plays a silent but significant role in how evacuation routes function. Consider the topographic features of your city. Low-lying areas are prone to flooding, turning what seems like a safe route into a watery trap. It's vital to understand which parts of your city are vulnerable and plan accordingly. Bridges and tunnels, while convenient, can become bottlenecks during an evacuation, susceptible to traffic jams that trap vehicles for hours. This knowledge helps you anticipate potential delays and adjust your plans to avoid these pitfalls. By integrating this understanding into your evacuation strategy, you can navigate your city with a sense of foresight, steering clear of areas that might hinder your escape.

Technology is your ally when it comes to real-time traffic data. Apps like Waze or Google Maps provide live updates on road conditions, allowing you to see which routes are congested and which remain clear. These apps harness the power of user data, offering insights that can guide your decisions in real time. City-specific traffic monitoring websites are also valuable resources, offering localized information that might not be available on global platforms. By using these tools, you stay one step ahead, adapting to conditions as they change. Access to this data means you're not just reacting to the situation but actively managing your path to safety.

Alternate routes are the unsung heroes of evacuation planning. Main roads can quickly become clogged, turning a straightforward exit into a nightmare. That's why mapping out secondary routes is crucial. Look for side streets that bypass main roads, offering a less congested path out of the city. These routes might take longer under normal circumstances, but during an evacuation, they can save precious time. Pedestrian paths are another option, especially in densely populated urban areas. In some cases, walking might be faster than driving, allowing you to bypass gridlocked streets entirely. By identifying these alternate routes in advance, you give yourself options, ensuring that even if your primary plan falters, you have a backup ready.

———

Activity: Route Mapping

Take some time to explore your city, focusing on potential evacuation routes. Use a map to mark official routes, noting any geographic features that might affect accessibility. Identify secondary routes, including side streets and pedestrian paths. This exercise not only familiarizes you with your city's layout but also empowers you to act with confidence during an evacuation. By understanding the intricacies of your city's evacuation network, you transform anxiety into action, preparing yourself to face any emergency with clarity and resolve.

———

6.3 EVACUATION DRILLS FOR CITY RESIDENTS

PICTURE THIS: you're at home, enjoying a quiet evening, when an alert sounds to signal an emergency evacuation. Panic sets in as you scramble to remember your plan. This scenario underscores the importance of regular evacuation drills. Practicing these drills isn't just a formality; it's a crucial step in ensuring you're ready when disaster strikes. Scheduling family evacuation practices can transform a chaotic rush into a coordinated effort. By designating roles and responsibilities, everyone knows what to do and where to go, reducing confusion and stress. But why stop at home? Community-wide drill events offer a broader scope, fostering a collective sense of preparedness. Imagine your entire building or neighborhood participating, turning a drill into a community event that strengthens bonds and boosts readiness.

The unpredictability of emergencies means you must prepare for a range of scenarios. Consider the unique challenges of a nighttime evacuation when darkness complicates navigation and heightens anxiety. Practice these drills in low-light conditions to familiarize yourself with the environment and develop strategies for safe movement. Pets and elderly family members add another layer of complexity. Ensuring their safety requires careful planning and practice. Designate someone to manage pets, ensuring carriers and leashes are ready. For elderly family members, plan for mobility assistance, whether it's a wheelchair or an extra set of hands. Patience is key during these drills. Evacuating under pressure can test anyone's composure, but staying calm and collected ensures a smoother process. Regular practice builds muscle memory, making your response instinctual when every second counts.

After conducting a drill, take time to evaluate its performance. Timed drills provide valuable insights into efficiency, highlighting areas where you might need to improve. Was there a delay in gathering supplies? Did confusion arise over designated meeting points? These questions guide your assessment, helping you pinpoint weaknesses in your plan. Post-drill debriefings offer an opportunity to discuss outcomes and gather feedback. Involve everyone in the conversation, from family members to neighbors, to gain diverse perspectives. These debriefings turn drills into learning experiences, highlighting strengths and areas for improvement. By openly discussing challenges and solutions, you create a culture of continuous improvement, ensuring your plan evolves to meet new needs and circumstances.

Feedback from drills is invaluable in refining your evacuation plan. Use it to address logistical issues encountered during practice. Perhaps a stairwell proved too narrow for swift movement, or communication breakdowns occurred over who was responsible for what. Adjust your plan to account for these obstacles, updating contact information and meeting points as necessary. Flexibility is your ally. By incorporating feedback and making necessary adjustments, you transform a static plan into a dynamic one capable of adapting to changing conditions. This iterative process ensures your readiness remains sharp, enabling you to face uncertainty with confidence and clarity.

———

Activity: Personal Evacuation Plan

Create a personal or family evacuation plan that includes checklists, routes, and maps for different situations. Start with evacuating the building, where the importance is on getting safely to
the street as quickly as possible. Then, brainstorm on how this
would be different if it was an evacuation of the neighborhood.
Finally, this needs to be applied to evacuate the city. Once you
have each situation planned, test your plans with drills. After
the drill, evaluate your performance and update the plan as
needed. You should also set a schedule for doing these drills
regularly to build muscle memory.

———

IN URBAN AREAS, where the landscape can change in an instant, the
importance of evacuation drills cannot be overstated. They transform
theoretical plans into practical actions, turning uncertainty into
preparedness. With regular practice, realistic scenarios, thorough eval-
uations, and responsive adjustments, you build a robust framework
that stands ready to guide you through any crisis.

6.4 NAVIGATING URBAN EVACUATIONS WITH FAMILY

In the hustle and bustle of urban life, planning for an evacuation can
feel overwhelming, especially when you consider the diverse needs of
your family. Each member has unique requirements that need
addressing to ensure a smooth evacuation process. For parents, childcare arrangements become a priority. It might mean designating a
parent or guardian to manage the children, ensuring they are
accounted for and secure. For families with members who have special
needs, accommodations must be thoughtfully integrated into the plan.
This could involve ensuring wheelchair accessibility or having a care-
giver on standby. Tailoring your evacuation plan to these individual

needs ensures everyone is safe and reduces the stress that often accompanies emergencies.

Establishing family meeting points is also a crucial element of any evacuation plan. Choose public landmarks that are easily identifiable, like a well-known park or a prominent building. These spots serve as beacons, guiding separated family members to a safe location. Additionally, consider setting safe zones away from high-risk areas. These zones should be easily accessible and have basic amenities if possible. By designating these meeting points beforehand, you provide a sense of direction and security, ensuring that even if chaos ensues, your family has a clear path to reunite and regroup.

A well-prepared family is one with carefully curated emergency kits. Each family member should have a kit tailored to their specific needs. For children, include age-appropriate items like snacks, toys, or comfort items that can soothe them during stressful times. Elderly members might require medications, important documents, and mobility aids. These kits are not just about survival; they offer comfort and assurance, making the evacuation process more manageable. By having these kits ready and easily accessible, you ensure that everyone has what they need when it matters most, easing the transition from home to safety.

Clear communication is the backbone of any successful evacuation. During emergencies, maintaining effective communication within the family is crucial. Mobile apps designed for emergency communication can also be invaluable, providing real-time updates and location sharing. Establishing a chain of command streamlines decision-making, ensuring that everyone knows who is making the calls. This clarity reduces confusion and helps keep the family more focused and united, even amidst the chaos of the evacuation. With a clear communication plan, your family moves as a cohesive unit, enhancing safety and coordination.

Pets are family, too, and their safety must be considered in your evacuation plans. Ensure you have pet carriers and leashes ready, as these will be essential for transporting animals safely. Prepare emergency pet supplies, including food, water, and any necessary medications. It's important to check in advance which shelters or evacuation sites allow pets so you're not caught off guard. Having a plan for your pets not only safeguards their well-being but also provides peace of mind for the entire family, knowing that all loved ones, furry or otherwise, are cared for and included in your preparations.

Navigating an urban evacuation with family is a complex task that requires foresight and attention to detail. By planning for diverse needs, establishing clear meeting points, preparing personalized kits, maintaining effective communication, and caring for pets, you create a robust framework that ensures everyone's safety. These plans are not just about logistics; they're about protecting what matters most.

Evacuating with family demands a thoughtful approach, balancing practical needs with emotional well-being. As we turn our focus to the broader community, we'll explore how collective efforts can enhance preparedness and foster resilience through unity and shared resources.

CHAPTER 7
COMMUNITY AND COLLECTIVE RESILIENCE

Picture this: a summer evening in the heart of the city, where a neighborhood block party is in full swing. Laughter echoes between buildings, and the tantalizing aroma of grilled food fills the air. This isn't just a celebration; it's a community coming together, strengthening bonds that could prove vital in times of crisis. Building neighborhood alliances is about more than just knowing who lives next door. It's about creating a network of support, ensuring that when disaster strikes, you're not alone. In the past, neighborhoods were naturally tight-knit, but urbanization has often left us feeling isolated despite living in close quarters. This chapter explores how to reconnect, turning our urban environments into bastions of resilience through collective effort and cooperation.

Fostering local connections begins with reaching out. Organizing regular block parties or gatherings serves as a perfect icebreaker. These events offer a relaxed setting to meet neighbors, share stories, and discuss common interests. The goal is to build a sense of familiarity and trust, laying the groundwork for mutual support. Creating a neighborhood contact list can further solidify these connections, providing a resource for quick communication during emergencies. Imagine having a list where everyone is just a call or text away, ready to offer a helping hand or share crucial information. This simple tool can make all the difference when time is of the essence.

In public safety, we say the worst time to exchange business cards with a colleague is during an emergency. The same can be said for meeting your neighbors.

Developing trust and cooperation among neighbors requires more than just occasional get-togethers. It involves sharing skills and resources and creating a community where everyone contributes to the collective well-being. One neighbor might have a knack for carpentry, another for gardening, and a third for first aid. By pooling these talents, you create a robust support system capable of tackling various challenges. Participating in community-building activities, such as neighborhood clean-ups or shared gardening projects, further strengthens these bonds. These activities foster a sense of pride and ownership, transforming a collection of individuals into a cohesive unit ready to face whatever challenges come their way.

Creating a neighborhood emergency plan is crucial for ensuring collective preparedness. Start by identifying the natural local leaders and coordinators who can act as points of contact during crises. These individuals should be approachable, trustworthy, and capable of rallying the community when needed. Establishing clear communication protocols is equally important, ensuring everyone knows how to convey information quickly and efficiently. Whether through group messaging apps, phone trees, or even old-fashioned flyers, having a plan in place ensures no one is left out in the cold when an emergency arises. This approach not only streamlines response efforts but also provides peace of mind, knowing there's a strategy in place for any eventuality.

Volunteer groups play a vital role in addressing specific preparedness and response tasks. Reach out to your local emergency manager to learn about the Community Emergency Response Team (CERT) program. This initiative trains volunteers in basic disaster response skills, from fire safety to search and rescue operations. Joining police or fire department auxiliary programs offers another avenue for involvement, providing additional training and resources. These programs are not just about learning new skills; they offer a chance to connect with like-minded individuals committed to community safety. First aid and medical support groups are also invaluable, providing essential care during emergencies when professional services might be over-whelmed. By forming these volunteer groups, you create a layer of resilience, ensuring your community is better equipped to handle crises.

Activity: Neighborhood Skills Inventory

Create a skills inventory for your neighborhood. List your own skills and resources first, then contact neighbors to learn what they can offer. Compile this information into a shared document or digital database accessible to all participating members. This inventory will serve as a valuable resource during emergencies, allowing you to quickly identify who can assist with specific tasks or needs.

BUILDING strong neighborhood alliances transforms urban living from a solitary experience to a supportive community endeavor. By fostering connections, developing trust, creating plans, and forming volunteer groups, you lay the foundation for a resilient neighborhood ready to tackle any challenge.

7.2 LEVERAGING LOCAL COMMUNITY RESOURCES

Imagine walking through your neighborhood and recognizing the untapped potential around you. Community centers, often bustling with activity, transform into vital shelters during emergencies. These spaces, familiar and welcoming, provide not only refuge but also a hub for coordination and information sharing. Local businesses, the back-bone of any urban area, can become critical allies in times of need. Picture a corner store supplying essentials like batteries and water or a café offering free Wi-Fi to keep residents connected. These assets, often taken for granted, play a crucial role in community preparedness. Identifying and utilizing these resources requires a proactive approach, reaching out and establishing relationships before a crisis hits. This foresight ensures you're not scrambling for help when it's needed most.

Engaging with local authorities is another cornerstone of effective community preparedness. Attending city council meetings might seem tedious, but these gatherings offer a direct line to decision-makers. They provide an opportunity to voice concerns, propose initiatives, and stay informed about local policies and emergency plans. Volunteering for local emergency management committees further deepens this engagement. These committees, often seeking diverse perspectives, welcome input from residents who understand their neighborhood's unique needs. By participating, you influence preparedness strategies and gain invaluable insights into how your city plans to respond to disasters. This collaboration fosters a sense of empowerment, knowing that you're actively contributing to the safety and resilience of your community.

Public spaces, scattered throughout urban landscapes, hold untapped potential as hubs for disaster preparedness. Libraries, typically associated with quiet study and learning, can host workshops on emergency readiness. These sessions, led by experts or experienced volunteers, equip residents with the knowledge and skills needed to face various crises. Imagine attending a workshop on first aid or emergency communication, leaving with not just information but practical skills that could save lives. Parks, often seen as mere recreational areas, can house emergency supply stations. These stations, stocked with essentials like food, blankets, and first-aid kits, offer quick access to resources during emergencies. By utilizing public spaces in these ways, communities create a network of support that's readily accessible to all residents.

Partnering with local organizations takes community resilience to another level. Non-profits, often deeply embedded in their communities, bring a wealth of resources and expertise. Collaborating with food banks ensures that emergency rations are available when supply chains falter. These partnerships provide a safety net, ensuring no one goes hungry during a crisis. Local health clinics, familiar with the community's health needs, can supply medical resources and personnel, enhancing the community's capacity to respond to health emergencies. These collaborations strengthen the fabric of community preparedness, weaving together various resources and skills to create a comprehensive support network. By building these partnerships, communities enhance their resilience, ensuring they're well-equipped to handle whatever challenges come their way.

7.3 ONLINE NETWORKS FOR URBAN PREPAREDNESS

In today's digital age, the power of online communities cannot be overstated, especially when it comes to urban preparedness. Imagine logging into a local Facebook group, a virtual gathering where neighbors share tips, resources, and updates about their community. These platforms offer an unparalleled opportunity to connect with fellow urban dwellers interested in disaster preparedness. They provide a space to exchange ideas and experiences, creating a sense of camaraderie and mutual support. Engaging with neighborhood forums further enhances this connection, offering a more structured environment for discussing specific topics related to emergency readiness. These forums often feature threads dedicated to preparedness, allowing members to ask questions, offer advice, and share valuable insights. By participating in these online communities, you gain access to a wealth of knowledge and resources that can enhance your preparedness efforts.

Sharing information and resources through online networks is a crucial aspect of building a resilient urban community. Imagine a scenario where someone posts an update about an upcoming preparedness workshop or shares a digital copy of their emergency plan. This act of sharing spreads awareness and encourages others to take similar steps. It fosters a culture of openness and collaboration, where individuals feel empowered to contribute and learn from one another. By regularly posting updates on community preparedness activities, you keep the conversation alive and ensure that preparedness remains a priority for all members. Sharing digital resources, such as emergency plans or checklists, further supports this collaborative effort, providing practical tools that others can adapt and implement in their own lives.

Coordinating virtual training sessions is another innovative way to educate community members on various preparedness topics. Imagine attending a webinar on first aid and CPR hosted by a local expert from the comfort of your home. These sessions provide a convenient and accessible platform for learning essential skills that could save lives during an emergency. Online workshops on emergency planning offer another avenue for education, guiding participants through the process of creating a comprehensive preparedness plan. These sessions can be recorded and shared, extending their reach and impact. By organizing and promoting virtual training sessions, you play a pivotal role in equipping your community with the knowledge and skills needed to respond effectively to crises.

The role of social media in providing real-time updates during emergencies cannot be overlooked. Platforms like X (Formerly Twitter) and Facebook become invaluable tools for disseminating information quickly and efficiently. However, it's essential to know how to identify authoritative sources to ensure the accuracy of the information you receive. Look for verified accounts of local authorities, emergency services, and reputable news organizations. These sources provide timely and reliable updates that can guide your response during an emergency. It's equally important to be vigilant about misinformation, which can spread rapidly on social media. Cross-referencing information with trusted sources helps you discern fact from fiction, ensuring you make informed decisions. Creating a community on social media accounts dedicated to alerts and updates allows you to share verified information with your network, keeping everyone informed and prepared.

Using platforms like Nextdoor for neighborhood-specific information further enhances your preparedness efforts. Nextdoor connects you with people living in your immediate vicinity, offering localized updates that are directly relevant to your situation. Imagine receiving a notification about a road closure due to flooding or a power outage affecting your block. This hyper-local focus ensures you're always up to date with the latest developments in your area. By actively participating in Nextdoor and similar platforms, you contribute to a well-informed community that's better equipped to handle emergencies.

7.4 COOPERATIVE STRATEGIES FOR SHARED SAFETY

Imagine walking through your neighborhood and knowing that every tool and skill you might need is just a few doors down. This isn't a utopian dream; it's a practical reality when communities pool their resources and skills. Establishing a community tool and equipment library is a straightforward yet transformative step toward enhancing collective safety. Picture a shared storage space where neighbors can borrow everything from ladders to power drills, reducing the need for each household to own their own. This approach not only saves money but also encourages collaboration and interaction among residents. Developing a skills inventory of residents complements this initiative. By identifying who has skills in carpentry, first aid, gardening, or even cooking, you create a living database that can be called upon in times of need. This inventory fosters a spirit of cooperation, ensuring that when emergencies arise, you're not facing them alone but as part of a well-prepared and resourceful community.

In addition to pooling resources, establishing community watch programs significantly enhances neighborhood safety and security. These programs aren't just about keeping an eye out for suspicious activities; they're about fostering a sense of solidarity and vigilance. Organizing regular patrols and meetings helps residents stay informed and engaged, creating a visible presence that deters potential threats. Collaborating with local law enforcement is key to the success of these programs. By working together, residents and police can share insights and strategies, ensuring that the community's specific concerns are addressed. This partnership not only improves safety but also builds trust between residents and law enforcement, fostering a sense of shared responsibility for the neighborhood's well-being.

Mutual aid networks take the concept of community support to another level, offering a framework for neighbors to assist each other during crises. These networks operate on the principle that everyone has something to offer, whether it's time, resources, or skills. Setting up a system for sharing food and supplies ensures that no one goes without during tough times. Imagine a neighborhood pantry where residents can drop off extra canned goods or pick up what they need, creating a cycle of giving and receiving that strengthens community ties. Coordinating childcare and elder care is another key aspect of mutual aid networks. By organizing a roster of volunteers who can assist with babysitting or checking in on elderly neighbors, you ensure that everyone is cared for, even when resources are stretched thin. This approach not only addresses immediate needs but also builds long-term resilience, creating a community that's prepared to face challenges together.

Specialized emergency task forces further enhance a community's ability to respond effectively to crises. Forming a communication task force ensures that accurate information is disseminated quickly, reducing confusion and panic. This team might be responsible for setting up a phone tree or managing a dedicated social media page, ensuring that everyone stays informed. A logistics team, on the other hand, focuses on managing supplies and distribution. Whether it's coordinating the delivery of emergency kits or organizing a food drive, this team ensures that resources are allocated efficiently and fairly. These task forces operate like the gears of a well-oiled machine, each playing a crucial role in maintaining the community's safety and stability during emergencies.

The strategies outlined here demonstrate the power of collective action in enhancing neighborhood safety and preparedness. By pooling resources, establishing watch programs, creating mutual aid networks, and developing specialized task forces, communities can transform their approach to emergency preparedness. These initiatives not only improve safety and resilience but also foster a sense of unity and cooperation, turning neighborhoods into supportive havens ready to face any challenge.

In the next chapter, we'll explore sustainable and eco-friendly preparedness strategies, delving into how green practices can further bolster urban resilience.

CHAPTER 8
SUSTAINABLE AND ECO-FRIENDLY PREPAREDNESS

Picture this: you're in the middle of a bustling city. The lights flicker and then go out. Silence falls, save for the hum of distant generators. As you fumble for your flashlight, you remember the solar charger you've stashed in your emergency kit. You step outside, and amidst the towering skyscrapers, a tiny panel begins converting sunlight into power. This isn't science fiction; it's a glimpse into how sustainable preparedness can transform urban living. In a world where environmental concerns grow, integrating eco-friendly practices into your emergency plan isn't just smart—it's essential. Let's explore how you can harness green energy solutions to stay prepared and protect the planet.

8.1 GREEN ENERGY SOLUTIONS FOR EMERGENCIES

When thinking about emergencies, power is often the first thing that comes to mind. In cities, where everything from elevators to internet connections relies on electricity, a power outage can bring life to a standstill.

Energy-efficient devices can be a cornerstone of sustainable preparedness. When every watt counts, devices that sip rather than guzzle power become invaluable. LED lanterns are a prime example, offering bright illumination with minimal energy use. Unlike traditional bulbs,

LEDs convert most of their energy into light, not heat, making them safer and more effective during emergencies. Pair them with energy-saving power banks, and you have a setup that keeps your space lit and your devices charged without draining your resources. These power banks are designed to hold their charge for extended periods, ensuring you always have backup power when you need it most. Investing in these efficient alternatives reduces your carbon footprint and enhances your preparedness, giving you peace of mind knowing you're ready for any situation.

Beyond individual solutions, community energy initiatives present an exciting opportunity to amplify your preparedness efforts. Picture a neighborhood where rooftops glisten with solar panels, collectively generating power for the community. This isn't just a dream; it's a reality in many urban areas where residents come together to install neighborhood solar panel systems. These initiatives not only reduce reliance on the grid but also foster a sense of community and shared responsibility. By pooling resources, neighborhoods can invest in shared battery storage systems, ensuring that excess energy is stored and available when needed. This collective approach to energy distribution not only enhances resilience during power outages but also promotes a culture of sustainability and cooperation. It's about transforming how we think about energy—not as a solitary endeavor but as a collective effort that benefits everyone involved.

Activity: Green Energy Exploration

Take a moment to explore your home and neighborhood for potential green energy solutions. Identify places where you could install solar chargers or panels. Consider joining a local community group focused on renewable energy projects. This exercise helps you visualize the potential for sustainable energy in your daily life and encourages you to incorporate these practices into your preparedness plan.

As you incorporate these green energy solutions into your emergency preparedness plan, remember that each step you take is a commitment to both safety and sustainability. By leveraging renewable energy, embracing efficient devices, and participating in community initiatives, you contribute to a more resilient and eco-friendly urban environment.

8.2 ECO-CONSCIOUS WATER STORAGE OPTIONS

Imagine waking up on a morning when the tap runs dry, and the anxiety of not knowing where your next glass of water *(or that first cup of coffee, in my case...)* will come from starts to set in. In our urban environments, where every drop counts, having a sustainable water storage plan is more than just a good idea—it's a necessity. One effective practice is rainwater harvesting, an ancient method that's making a modern comeback. Picture a sleek rain barrel positioned under your gutter, quietly collecting water from the morning's drizzle. With every inch of rain on a 1,000-square-foot roof yielding over 600 gallons of water, you're tapping into a natural, free resource that can significantly reduce your dependency on city water supplies. These systems aren't just practical; they're environmentally friendly, reducing stormwater runoff that can lead to urban flooding. Plus, they offer an independent water supply that's perfect for non-potable uses like flushing toilets or watering plants, cutting down on your water bill in the process.

When it comes to storing water for consumption, reusable containers are your best bet. They stand as a sustainable alternative to single-use plastic bottles, offering both environmental benefits and practicality. Consider investing in high-quality, BPA-free containers that are designed for long-term use. You can fill these with tap water or rainwater (after purifying it, of course) and store them in a cool, dark place to maintain freshness. The key is to regularly rotate your stored water to ensure it remains drinkable. By doing so, you're not just preparing for emergencies; you're adopting a lifestyle that reflects a commitment to sustainability.

To ensure that your stored water is safe to drink, natural filtration methods come into play. DIY charcoal water filters are a simple yet effective solution. Charcoal, with its porous structure, acts like a magnet for impurities, trapping particles and improving taste. You can easily make a charcoal filter using activated carbon, sand, and gravel layered in a container. Ceramic filtration systems offer another layer of protection. These systems, often used in developing regions, filter out bacteria and protozoa, providing safe drinking water without the need for chemicals. Using these natural methods not only ensures your water is clean but also reduces reliance on bottled water, aligning with eco-friendly practices.

In an urban setting, where resources can quickly dwindle during a crisis, optimizing water usage is crucial. Implementing water rationing plans ensures that every drop is used wisely. Start by calculating your household's daily water needs and create a plan that allocates a specific amount for each person. This plan should prioritize drinking, cooking, and basic hygiene while also considering pets and plants. Low-flow fixtures, such as aerated faucets and showerheads, can dramatically reduce water consumption without sacrificing performance. These fixtures can cut water use by up to 50%, making them a smart investment for both everyday use and emergency situations. By adopting these measures, you're not just conserving water; you're making a conscious choice to protect one of our most precious resources.

On a larger scale, engaging in community water conservation efforts amplifies the impact of individual actions. Imagine a neighborhood where each home has a rainwater collection system, collectively reducing the demand on municipal water supplies. Shared purification systems could also be implemented, where a community pool of resources allows for the treatment of larger volumes of water. This approach fosters a sense of community and ensures that everyone has access to safe water during emergencies. By participating in such initiatives, you're contributing to a culture of sustainability and resilience, where neighbors support each other in times of need.

Water, often taken for granted, becomes a focal point in emergency preparedness. By adopting sustainable storage practices, utilizing natural filtration, optimizing usage, and engaging in community efforts, you're preparing for the unexpected and promoting a responsible approach to resource management. This mindset shift not only prepares you for the challenges of urban living but also cultivates a lifestyle that respects and values the environment.

8.3 SUSTAINABLE FOOD SUPPLIES FOR URBANITES

Imagine strolling through a vibrant farmers' market, the air filled with the scent of fresh herbs and ripe fruits. Supporting local agriculture by purchasing from these markets not only enhances your emergency stockpile with fresh produce but also strengthens your community's economy. Farmers' markets offer a variety of organic foods that are not only fresher but often boast a smaller carbon footprint than their supermarket counterparts. And there's something inherently satisfying about knowing exactly where your food comes from. Community-supported agriculture (CSA) programs take this a step further. By subscribing to a CSA, you receive regular boxes of seasonal produce, directly supporting farmers and enjoying a diverse range of items that can be preserved or consumed immediately. This direct-to-consumer model reduces food miles, the distance food travels from farm to plate, making it a more sustainable choice. And in terms of preparedness, you are shortening the supply chain. Instead of waiting for fresh food to travel across the country, you are leveraging a local resource.

Urban gardening is another avenue to explore. Why rely on someone else to provide you with fresh food during an emergency when you can provide your own? Even if your living space is limited to a small balcony, container gardening allows you to grow your own vegetables and herbs, bringing a touch of green to your urban environment. Imagine stepping onto your balcony to pluck fresh basil leaves for tonight's dinner or harvesting cherry tomatoes that burst with flavor. Rooftop vegetable gardens are another exciting option. They transform underutilized spaces into productive green rooftops, providing fresh produce and improving urban air quality. These gardens are more than just a food source; they offer a sense of accomplishment and a deeper connection to the food you consume. Whether it's a few pots on a balcony or a sprawling rooftop garden, urban gardening empowers you to take control of part of your food supply, reducing reliance on external sources and enhancing food security.

When it comes to stocking your emergency kit, foods with long shelf lives should be a priority. Dried fruits and nuts are excellent choices, offering a nutrient-rich snack that remains fresh for months. They provide essential vitamins and minerals, ensuring you maintain a balanced diet during emergencies. Vacuum-sealed grains and legumes are another must-have. These staples are not only versatile but also store well, making them a reliable source of protein and energy. Picture a pantry lined with jars of dried beans, rice, and lentils, each ready to be transformed into a nourishing meal at a moment's notice. By focusing on foods with extended shelf lives, you create a sustainable food supply that can withstand the test of time.

Supporting local and organic food sources, engaging in urban gardening, and focusing on long-lasting foods are steps you can take to enhance your food security. These options connect you to your community and the environment, offering a sustainable approach to preparedness. As you consider these options, consider how they fit into your lifestyle and how they can enrich your daily life. Each choice you make contributes to a more resilient and sustainable future.

8.4 REDUCING WASTE IN PREPAREDNESS PLANNING

In our fast-paced urban lives, it's easy to overlook the waste generated by our daily habits, especially when planning for emergencies. We all generate A LOT of waste daily, and we rely on city services to remove that waste. Now, imagine what would happen if the garbage truck couldn't come for several days. The accumulation of garbage quickly becomes a nuisance and a public health problem.

Adopting a zero-waste mindset can transform how you approach disaster preparedness, benefiting you, your community during the emergency, and the environment. Consider your emergency kit. Instead of single-use plastics, opt for reusable containers to store supplies. Glass jars or metal tins work well for everything from food to first-aid items. They're not just durable; they also reduce your environmental impact and the waste you generate during an emergency. By swapping out plastic bags for cloth pouches or beeswax wraps, you cut down on disposable waste while keeping your supplies organized and accessible. Avoiding single-use plastics isn't just about environmental responsibility; it's about creating a sustainable system that you can maintain long-term. This approach ensures your preparedness doesn't come at the cost of the planet's health.

Repurposing and recycling materials further enhance your preparedness kit's sustainability. Take old clothing, for instance. Those worn-out jeans can be upcycled into sturdy emergency blankets or used as makeshift bandages. With a little creativity, they become invaluable tools, ready to support you when needed. And don't underestimate the power of recycled paper. Use it for emergency insulation by crumpling it up and placing it between you and the cold, reducing the need for new resources. This practice not only saves money but also fosters a mindset of resourcefulness and innovation. By looking at used materials through a new lens, you create a preparedness plan that is as eco-friendly as it is effective. This shift encourages you to see potential in what others might discard, transforming waste into resources.

Community initiatives can amplify individual efforts, fostering a collective approach to waste reduction. Imagine participating in a community composting program where neighbors gather to turn organic waste into nutrient-rich compost. This initiative not only reduces waste but also provides a valuable resource for urban gardens, supporting local food production. Swap events are another exciting opportunity. Picture a gathering where community members exchange reusable supplies, from tools to clothing, reducing the need for new purchases and fostering a spirit of sharing and cooperation. These events build connections, transforming waste reduction into a social endeavor. By collaborating with your community, you contribute to a culture of sustainability and resilience where everyone benefits from reduced waste and increased resources.

By integrating these waste-reduction strategies into your preparedness planning, you create a system that respects both the environment and your urban lifestyle and doesn't attract every rat on the block. It's about finding balance, where being prepared doesn't mean compromising on sustainability. As you move forward, consider how these principles can enhance not just your emergency plan but your daily life, fostering a mindset of responsibility and innovation. This chapter ties into the broader theme of sustainable living, reflecting a commitment to preparedness that is both practical and planet-friendly. In the next chapter, we'll explore how to build resilience through psychological preparedness, focusing on mental strategies that complement the physical preparations we've discussed.

CHAPTER 9
PSYCHOLOGICAL PREPAREDNESS IN CRISIS

t's a bustling city morning, the air filled with the symphony of honking horns and chatter. Suddenly, the ground shakes, and chaos ensues. In an instant, the familiar becomes foreign, and stress levels surge. This is the reality of urban disasters, where the noise and unpredictability can leave you feeling overwhelmed. Understanding and managing stress in these moments becomes crucial. Stress isn't just an emotional response; it's a physical reaction that can cloud judgment and hinder your ability to act. In the midst of chaos, knowing how to recognize and manage stress can make all the difference. All the kits and plans in the world won't help you if you aren't mentally and emotionally prepared for the chaos.

9.1 MANAGING STRESS IN A CRISIS

Stress in a crisis can manifest in various ways. Loud noises and chaos, prevalent in urban environments, can trigger heightened anxiety. The sound of sirens, the commotion of crowded streets, and the relentless pace of city life can amplify stress levels. Lack of information or uncertainty further exacerbates this stress. When you're unsure of what's happening or what to do next, your mind fills in the gaps with worst-case scenarios. Recognizing these stress triggers is the first step in regaining control. Awareness allows you to anticipate your reactions and implement strategies to manage them effectively.

Implementing stress reduction techniques can provide relief in high-pressure situations. Deep breathing exercises, for example, can help calm your nervous system. Inhale deeply through your nose, hold for a moment, and then exhale slowly through your mouth. This simple act can slow your heart rate and bring clarity to your thoughts. Progressive muscle relaxation is another effective method. By tensing and then relaxing different muscle groups, you can release built-up tension and induce a state of calm. These techniques are easy to practice and can be done anywhere, making them ideal for the unpredictability of urban crises.

Creating a personalized stress management plan equips you with tools to navigate difficult moments. Start by identifying calming activities and practices that resonate with you. This could be listening to music, journaling, or taking a short walk. Incorporating these activities into your routine ensures you have an outlet for stress whenever needed. Setting aside "decompression" time is equally important. Dedicate a few minutes each day to unwind and disconnect from stressors. Whether it's enjoying a cup of tea or indulging in a favorite hobby, these moments of peace can recharge your mental reserves. Having a plan in place provides a roadmap for managing stress, ensuring you're prepared for whatever comes your way.

Leveraging support systems is vital in alleviating stress during crises. Building a network of trusted friends and family offers emotional and practical support. These connections provide a sense of security and reassurance, reminding you that you're not alone in facing challenges. Participating in support groups can also be beneficial. These groups offer a platform to share experiences and gain insights from others who understand what you're going through. Engaging with a community of peers fosters a sense of belonging and resilience, enhancing your ability to cope with stress.

————

Activity: Stress Inventory Exercise

Take a moment to conduct a stress inventory. Reflect on recent stressful experiences and identify common triggers. Consider how you typically respond to stress and which techniques have been effective in the past. Document your findings in a journal or digital note. This exercise will help you recognize patterns and develop strategies for managing stress in future crises.

————

IN THE FAST-PACED URBAN LANDSCAPE, where disasters can strike unexpectedly, managing stress becomes an essential skill. By recognizing triggers, implementing reduction techniques, and leveraging support systems, you can navigate crises with confidence and resilience.

9.2 MINDFULNESS TECHNIQUES FOR URBAN DWELLERS

Living in a city often feels like being in the middle of a whirlwind, with sights, sounds, and sensations bombarding you from all directions. It's easy to become reactive, letting stress dictate your response to the chaos. This is where mindfulness steps in, offering a way to anchor yourself amid the storm. Mindfulness is all about staying present, focusing on the here and now without judgment. It encourages you to notice your surroundings, thoughts, and feelings without being swept away by them. For urban dwellers, this practice can be transformative during a crisis. By reducing reactive tendencies, mindfulness allows you to respond thoughtfully rather than impulsively, keeping you calm and centered even when everything else is in turmoil. This presence of mind doesn't just help in times of stress; it enhances your daily life, making you more aware and appreciative of each moment.

Incorporating mindfulness into a bustling urban lifestyle doesn't require hours of meditation or solitude. Instead, it can be seamlessly integrated into your routine, starting with simple exercises. Five-minute meditation sessions are a great place to start. Find a quiet spot, sit comfortably, and focus on your breath. Notice the rise and fall of your chest and let thoughts come and go without clinging to them. This short exercise can be surprisingly effective, offering a quick reset for your mind. Mindful walking is another exercise well-suited to city life. As you walk, pay attention to each step, the sensation of your feet touching the ground, and the rhythm of your movement. Observe your surroundings without judgment, noticing the play of light and shadow, the rustle of leaves, or the hum of traffic. These exercises require no special equipment or setting, making them accessible wherever you are.

Mindfulness can also be woven into daily activities, turning routine tasks into moments of presence. Take eating, for example. Rather than rushing through meals, practice mindful eating by savoring each bite and noticing the flavors and textures. This simple shift transforms a mundane activity into a sensory experience, grounding you in the present. Similarly, practice breathing mindfulness during your commute. Whether you're on a crowded train or stuck in traffic, focus on your breath. Notice its natural rhythm and use it as an anchor amidst the noise and bustle. These practices don't add time to your schedule; they transform the time you already have, enhancing awareness and calmness.

In the digital age, technology can be a valuable ally in cultivating mindfulness, offering tools and resources to support your practice. Mindfulness apps like Headspace or Calm provide guided meditations tailored to various needs, from stress reduction to sleep improvement. These apps make mindfulness accessible, offering short sessions that fit into any schedule. Guided meditation podcasts are another resource, providing audio sessions you can listen to during your commute or while relaxing at home. These tools offer guidance and structure, making it easier to maintain a consistent practice. They also serve as reminders to pause and breathe, even on the busiest days.

Engaging with these apps and podcasts helps reinforce the habit of mindfulness, providing support and inspiration as you cultivate your practice.

Incorporating mindfulness into urban life is about finding balance and creating space for presence amid the chaos. By practicing mindfulness, you cultivate a state of awareness that enhances your ability to navigate challenges with clarity and composure. This practice empowers you to embrace each moment fully and respond to crises with a calm and focused mind.

9.3 EMOTIONAL RESILIENCE AND EMERGENCY SITUATIONS

The city never stops. Its rhythm is constant, even when chaos strikes. In these moments, emotional resilience becomes your foundation. It starts with building emotional awareness. Take a moment to consider your feelings during past emergencies. Perhaps you felt fear, anger, or confusion. Journaling is an excellent way to track these emotional states. By putting pen to paper, you gain insight into your responses, identifying patterns and triggers. Reflection allows you to process these emotions and understand how they influence your actions. This awareness is powerful. It transforms unpredictable reactions into intentional responses, equipping you to handle future crises with clarity.

Once you understand your emotions, the next step is to strengthen your coping mechanisms. Cognitive reframing techniques are invaluable here. They involve shifting your perspective on a situation and turning negative thoughts into positive ones. For instance, instead of viewing a crisis as insurmountable, see it as a challenge that tests your resilience. This mindset shift empowers you to face difficulties head-on. Positive affirmations and self-talk further bolster your emotional resilience. By repeating uplifting statements, you reinforce your inner strength and confidence. These affirmations remind you that you possess the tools to navigate any storm, bolstering your emotional fortitude.

Developing adaptive thinking is crucial for maintaining flexibility and resilience. In a city, change is constant. Embracing this change, rather than resisting it, prepares you for the unknown. Accept that uncertainty is part of life and set realistic expectations for yourself. This mindset encourages adaptability, allowing you to pivot and adjust as circumstances evolve. Rather than being thrown off balance by unexpected events, you become a master of adaptation, ready to tackle any situation with poise. Adaptive thinking fosters resilience, ensuring you remain steady even when the world around you shifts.

Emotional self-regulation is the final piece of the puzzle. It involves practicing techniques that help you control your emotional responses during high-stress events. Grounding techniques are particularly effective. They anchor you to the present, helping you focus on the here and now. One simple method is the "5-4-3-2-1" technique: identify five things you can see, four you can touch, three you can hear, two you can smell, and one you can taste. This exercise redirects your attention from overwhelming emotions to tangible sensations, calming your mind. Visualization exercises are another powerful tool. Picture a place where you feel safe and relaxed. Immerse yourself in this mental image, absorbing the peace it brings. These strategies provide a mental escape from stress, allowing you to regain control and maintain composure.

Urban life is fast-paced and unrelenting, but it offers opportunities for growth and resilience. By cultivating emotional awareness, bolstering coping mechanisms, and practicing regulation techniques, you prepare yourself for whatever challenges come your way. In the city, where unpredictability is the norm, emotional resilience becomes your most valuable asset. It's your anchor, your guide, and your strength.

9.4 OVERCOMING FEAR AND ANXIETY IN DISASTERS

Fear is a primal response deeply rooted in our biology. When disaster looms, your body reacts instinctively, preparing to either fight the threat or flee from danger. This fight-or-flight response triggers a cascade of physiological changes. Your heart rate increases, your palms sweat, and your senses heighten. It's your body's way of gearing up for action. While useful in genuine threats, this response can overwhelm when the threat isn't physical, leading to anxiety. Anxiety manifests in various ways. You might feel a knot in your stomach, a racing mind, or a sense of impending doom. These symptoms can cloud judgment, making it difficult to think clearly. Recognizing these responses helps you understand that they're natural, even if they're uncomfortable.

Challenging negative thoughts is crucial in managing anxiety during disasters. Our minds often jump to catastrophic thinking, imagining the worst possible outcomes. This pattern amplifies fear, leaving you paralyzed rather than proactive. Start by questioning these thoughts. Are they based on facts or assumptions? Often, catastrophic thoughts crumble under scrutiny, revealing less daunting realities. Replace these thoughts with positive alternatives. Instead of thinking, "I can't handle this," remind yourself of past challenges you've overcome. This positive reframing shifts your focus from helplessness to capability, empowering you to take action.

Cultivating a fear-resilient mindset involves focusing on what you can control. Disasters bring chaos, but within that chaos, there are elements you can manage. Prepare an emergency kit, know your evacuation routes, and have a communication plan. These actions build confidence, reminding you that while you can't control everything, you're not powerless. Preparation doesn't eliminate fear, but it does minimize it, providing a mental anchor amid uncertainty. Confidence grows from knowing you've done what you can. This mindset doesn't deny fear but acknowledges it without letting it dictate actions.

Sometimes, the fear and anxiety experienced during disasters exceed what you can manage alone. In these moments, seeking professional help is not just wise—it's necessary. Mental health professionals offer expertise in navigating complex emotions and providing tools and support tailored to your needs. Therapy or counseling sessions create a safe space to explore fears, understand their roots, and develop coping strategies. These professionals guide you toward clarity and resilience, helping you process emotions constructively. There's no shame in seeking help. It's a courageous step toward well-being.

As you navigate fear and anxiety, remember that you're not alone. Many share these feelings, and reaching out for support can make a world of difference. Whether through professional help or personal connections, building a support network strengthens your capacity to face disasters with resilience and courage. Fear may be a part of the experience, but it doesn't define it. With understanding, preparation, and support, you can confidently face the uncertainties of urban living.

In the next chapter, we'll explore real-life scenarios that test these skills, equipping you with practical insights into effectively navigating urban crises.

CHAPTER 10
REAL-LIFE URBAN DISASTER SCENARIOS

n the thick of an urban landscape, where life pulses with a rhythm all its own, the unexpected can strike with a force that leaves cities reeling. Imagine a sudden deluge, turning streets into waterways and neighborhoods into islands. This isn't just a scene from a disaster movie; it's a reality that many urban dwellers have faced. Floods can upend lives, disrupt communities, and challenge the very infrastructure that supports city living. Yet, within these harrowing events lie lessons in resilience and preparedness, providing insights into how urban communities can withstand and recover from nature's fiercest tests.

10.1 CASE STUDY: URBAN FLOOD RESPONSE

Let's dive into Hurricane Harvey, which slammed into Houston in 2017, leaving a trail of devastation in its wake. Houston, a sprawling metropolis, found itself submerged under record-breaking rainfall. The city, built on a flat plain with a complex network of bayous, was particularly vulnerable. As floodwaters rose, the challenges of urban planning and infrastructure became starkly visible. Flood-prone areas saw unprecedented damage as drainage systems were overwhelmed. The sheer volume of water turned highways into rivers, isolating communities and stranding residents. Yet, amid this chaos, stories of survival and community spirit emerged, showing how resilience and preparedness played pivotal roles in the city's response.

In examining the 2012 New York City floods sparked by Hurricane Sandy, we see another city grappling with nature's wrath. New York, a city defined by its iconic skyline and bustling streets, faced an unexpected adversary. The storm surge flooded subways, knocked out power, and left neighborhoods in darkness. The city's unique geography, with its proximity to the coast and reliance on underground transport systems, amplified the impact. These events highlighted the vulnerabilities of urban infrastructure but also showcased the resilience of its people. New Yorkers, known for their tenacity, banded together to navigate the challenges, demonstrating the power of community in times of crisis.

Effective flood mitigation measures have become a critical focus in urban planning. One such strategy involves the deployment of portable flood barriers. These barriers, designed to be quickly erected in vulnerable areas, act as a temporary shield against rising waters. During Harvey, these barriers helped protect critical infrastructure and minimize damage to essential services. Efficient use of public warning systems also proved vital. Alerting residents early allowed for timely evacuations and preparations, reducing the risk of harm. The importance of clear, concise communication cannot be overstated, as it empowers individuals to take informed action.

Community involvement has emerged as a cornerstone of successful flood response and recovery. In Houston, grassroots volunteer efforts played an essential role. Residents came together, filling sandbags and working tirelessly to protect homes and businesses. This collective action exemplified the strength of neighborly bonds in the face of adversity. Neighborhood coordination for evacuation assistance further highlighted community solidarity. Organized efforts ensured that the most vulnerable, including the elderly and those without transportation, received the help they needed. These community-based approaches reinforced the idea that resilience is a shared endeavor built on cooperation and trust.

Long-term recovery strategies are crucial for rebuilding after a flood, ensuring that cities not only recover but also emerge stronger. Infrastructure improvements to prevent future flooding are a key aspect of this recovery. In flood-prone areas, enhancing drainage systems and elevating roads can mitigate the risk of future inundations. Government grants for home elevation projects offer financial support to help residents adapt their properties to withstand future floods. These initiatives not only protect individual homes but also contribute to the overall resilience of the community. By investing in these long-term solutions, cities can better prepare for the challenges of the future, safeguarding both lives and property in the face of an uncertain climate.

10.2 LESSONS FROM PAST EARTHQUAKES

When you think about earthquakes, the images that flash through your mind are often dramatic and unsettling. Buildings swaying, streets cracking, and an entire city grappling with forces beyond control. Take the 1994 Northridge earthquake in Los Angeles, for instance. This seismic event, with a magnitude of 6.7, shook the San Fernando Valley and sent shockwaves well beyond its borders. The quake exposed vulnerabilities in what was thought to be robust infrastructure. Steel construction using beams and columns, once considered reliable, buckled under the stress. This surprising failure prompted a reevaluation of building codes and spurred innovations to enhance resilience. Lessons from this quake highlighted the need for retrofitting older buildings to withstand seismic activity. Retrofitting involves strengthening the structural elements of a building, like adding steel braces or base isolators, to absorb and dissipate seismic energy. This process, though costly, can significantly reduce the risk of collapse during future quakes. The Northridge experience taught us that proactive measures could save lives and prevent economic loss.

Fast-forward to 2011 in Christchurch, New Zealand, and the story is eerily familiar yet unique. Here, a magnitude 6.3 earthquake devastated the city, leaving behind a landscape of fallen structures and fractured streets. Christchurch's experience illustrated the importance of considering local geology in urban planning. The city, built on soft, sandy soils, experienced liquefaction—a process where the ground temporarily loses its solidity during a quake. Buildings sank, roads buckled, and utility lines were severed. This event underscored the need for urban planners to account for soil conditions in their designs. It also emphasized the value of improving bridge and road durability, ensuring critical infrastructure can withstand seismic shocks. Christchurch's response included revising building codes to demand more rigorous standards, focusing on flexibility and strength. These efforts aimed to prevent similar devastation in the future, showcasing resilience as a dynamic process involving learning and adaptation.

Emergency response effectiveness can make or break a city's recovery after an earthquake. Rapid deployment of search and rescue teams is crucial. In the chaos following a quake, these teams are the first line of defense, saving lives and stabilizing the situation. Their swift actions during the Northridge quake minimized casualties and facilitated a quicker recovery. Community-led first aid stations also played a significant role. These grassroots efforts, often organized by local residents, provided immediate medical care to those in need, bridging the gap until professional help arrived. Such initiatives highlight the importance of community involvement in disaster response. The ability to mobilize quickly and efficiently can significantly impact the outcome of a crisis, underscoring the need for preparedness and training at all levels.

Beyond the physical toll, earthquakes leave deep psychological and social scars on urban populations. Post-traumatic stress is a common aftermath as individuals grapple with the sudden loss of stability and safety. Communities may struggle to regain a sense of normalcy, especially if faced with significant destruction. Support networks become vital in these times, providing comfort and a sense of solidarity. The role of mental health services in recovery cannot be overstated. These services offer counseling and support, helping individuals process their trauma and rebuild their lives. Community support networks, such as local groups and online forums, also provide a platform for sharing experiences and fostering resilience. By coming together, individuals find strength and hope, reinforcing the idea that recovery extends beyond physical rebuilding.

10.3 A CITY-WIDE BLACKOUT

Imagine the heart of a vibrant city suddenly plunged into darkness. The hum of electricity silenced, streetlights extinguished, and the familiar glow of screens vanished. This was the reality during the 2003 Northeast blackout, which left New York City and much of the surrounding areas in the dark. The sudden loss of power was a jarring reminder of our dependency on electricity. As the blackout stretched over hours, people found themselves on the streets, sharing stories and resources, making the best of an unforeseen situation. Fast-forward to 2019, when Caracas, Venezuela, experienced a blackout that lasted days. The city, already grappling with economic challenges, faced an even more dire situation. Residents were cut off from news, basic services crumbled, and the absence of light was a constant reminder of vulnerability. Yet, both instances provided valuable insights into human adaptability and the power of community.

During these extended blackouts, residents developed creative coping strategies. In New York, people gathered in parks for community cooking, sharing food and stories, and turning a crisis into a community event. Neighbors opened their homes, offering warmth and companionship. Alternative light sources, like candles and battery-powered lanterns, became vital. In Caracas, people turned to the sun, using daylight to cook and conduct essential activities. Makeshift stoves appeared on balconies, and open spaces became communal kitchens. It wasn't just about survival; it was about finding ways to adapt and maintain a sense of normalcy in unusual circumstances. These experiences highlight the importance of flexibility and creativity in the face of adversity.

Technology, often blamed for disconnecting us, proved invaluable during these crises. In New York, local radio stations became lifelines, offering updates and information amidst the silence. People tuned in on battery-powered radios, clinging to the familiar voices as links to the outside world. Social media platforms, although limited by the lack of power, still managed to serve as channels for updates when service was sporadically available. Residents used their phones sparingly, preserving battery life for critical communication. In Caracas, social media played a crucial role in organizing community responses. Updates on available resources, safe zones, and community gatherings circulated, keeping people connected despite the chaos. These platforms underscored the importance of communication and the role technology plays in maintaining connections even when everything else fails.

Once the lights flickered back on, the recovery process began, offering lessons that would shape future responses. Infrastructure upgrades became a priority, as aging grids and outdated systems were identified as weak points. In the Northeast, power companies invested in modernizing grids to prevent future outages, focusing on resilience and reliability. Caracas, faced with a more complex set of challenges, began to explore alternative energy sources and community-based power solutions. The blackouts sparked discussions on energy conservation and sustainability, prompting community workshops that educated residents on how to reduce consumption and prepare for potential future outages. These workshops emphasized practical steps, such as using energy-efficient appliances and adopting solar power where feasible. The lessons learned during these blackouts highlighted the importance of both individual preparedness and collective action, encouraging communities to come together and find solutions that ensure resilience and sustainability.

In the heart of darkness, cities found light in their people's resilience. These blackout experiences served as stark reminders of how fragile modern life can be, yet they also showcased the strength and adaptability inherent in urban communities. From sharing meals by candlelight to using technology creatively, these moments of crisis became opportunities for growth and learning. They reminded us that while power lines might fail, the human spirit continues to shine brightly.

10.4 CIVIL UNREST AND URBAN PREPAREDNESS

Civil unrest can transform a bustling city into a scene of chaos, where the familiar becomes unpredictable, and daily life grinds to a halt. Understanding the dynamics of such unrest is crucial for urban preparedness. The 1992 Los Angeles riots serve as a stark reminder of how quickly tensions can escalate. Triggered by the acquittal of police officers in the Rodney King trial, the riots erupted into widespread violence and looting. The city, known for its sprawling freeways and diverse neighborhoods, found itself divided and tense. Streets that once buzzed with activity fell silent as businesses shuttered and residents took cover. This civil discord exposed underlying racial and economic tensions, highlighting the fragile social fabric that can unravel under pressure. Then, in 2020, amid the already tense world of COVID-19, similar levels of First Amendment activities and civil unrest unfolded across the nation following the death of George Floyd.

The 2019 Hong Kong protests, fueled by political grievances and demands for greater autonomy, illustrated how prolonged unrest can strain a city. Demonstrators clashed with police, and public spaces became battlegrounds for conflicting ideologies. Situations like this that have played out across the Middle East and South America have ended in complete changes to national leadership. In the U.S., issues like reproductive rights, racial equality, and political division have created a very tenuous environment that frequently sees civil unrest unfold quickly. These events underscored the importance of understanding the triggers and dynamics of urban unrest, revealing how swiftly grievances can ignite and spread, turning cities into flashpoints of confrontation.

Community preparedness and response strategies are vital in navigating the complexities of civil unrest. Establishing robust communication networks for safety alerts provides a lifeline for residents, enabling them to stay informed and make quick decisions. In Los Angeles, the flow of information was crucial in helping people avoid hot spots and stay safe. Neighborhood watch groups also play a significant role, acting as the eyes and ears of the community. These groups foster a sense of solidarity, encouraging neighbors to look out for one another amidst the chaos. In Hong Kong, grassroots organizations emerged as key players, coordinating efforts to provide medical aid and legal assistance to those caught in the turmoil. These community-based initiatives demonstrate the power of collective action, highlighting how residents can band together to protect their neighborhoods and ensure mutual support. By nurturing these networks, communities can build resilience, transforming themselves from passive observers into proactive participants in their own safety.

The impact of civil unrest on urban infrastructure is profound and widespread. Public transportation systems, often the arteries of a city, can become targets or casualties of unrest. In Los Angeles, buses and trains were halted, leaving many without a means of escape. The strain on emergency services and law enforcement was palpable, as resources were stretched thin to maintain order and respond to emergencies. Police and fire departments faced unprecedented challenges, navigating the dual demands of protecting citizens and restoring peace. Similarly, during the Hong Kong protests, transportation networks were disrupted, affecting daily commutes and access to essential services. These disruptions underscore the vulnerability of urban infrastructure, highlighting the need for contingency planning and the fortification of essential services. As cities become more interconnected, ensuring the resilience of transportation and emergency systems is paramount to maintaining stability during times of unrest.

Promoting peaceful conflict resolution is a critical component in preventing and mitigating civil unrest. Community dialogue initiatives offer a platform for addressing grievances, fostering understanding, and building bridges between disparate groups. In the aftermath of the Los Angeles riots, community leaders launched dialogue forums, bringing together diverse voices to discuss underlying issues and seek common ground. Engaging with local leaders and activists is another effective strategy, as they possess valuable insights into the needs and concerns of their communities. By involving these stakeholders in the decision-making process, cities can develop more inclusive policies that address the root causes of unrest rather than merely treating symptoms. In Hong Kong, efforts to promote dialogue and understanding faced challenges, but they underscored the importance of open communication and the need to address societal tensions proactively. These peace-building efforts highlight the value of collaboration and communication in fostering stability, illustrating how cities can become catalysts for change and understanding.

Civil unrest is a complex and multifaceted challenge that requires a proactive approach. By understanding its dynamics, fostering community resilience, and promoting peaceful resolution, urban areas can navigate these turbulent times with greater confidence and cohesion. In the next chapter, we'll explore how to foster a preparedness mindset, building on the lessons learned from these real-life scenarios to ensure readiness for whatever challenges may come.

CHAPTER 11
FOSTERING A PREPAREDNESS MINDSET

Picture yourself in the middle of an ordinary urban morning. The city hums with its usual rhythm. People rush to work, coffee shops buzz, and traffic lights flicker in their synchronized dance. Yet, somewhere in the back of your mind, there's a nudge—a reminder of the unpredictability that shadows urban life. What if today was the day when routine turned into chaos? This thought shouldn't paralyze you with fear but motivate you to take control. Shifting from reaction to pro-action in disaster preparedness is about embracing the power of foresight and turning uncertainty into an opportunity for readiness.

Understanding the importance of proactive preparedness is the first step. Think about the stress and anxiety that often accompany emergencies. They can be reduced significantly with a little planning. When you know you've taken steps to prepare, your confidence grows. You become someone who can handle unexpected situations with calm and composure. It's like having an insurance policy for peace of mind. You're not just reacting to what happens; you're equipped to face it head-on. This confidence isn't just about surviving; it's about thriving in the face of adversity.

Setting clear preparedness goals is essential. Start by creating a timeline for assembling your emergency kit. Break it down into manageable tasks that you can tackle each month. Maybe this month, focus on gathering essential food supplies. Next month, work on collecting first-aid items. By setting these monthly objectives, you're not just gathering supplies; you're building skills. Consider adding skill-building activities to your goals, like learning first aid or attending a community preparedness workshop. Each step brings you closer to a state of readiness that feels achievable and empowering.

Developing a strategic preparedness plan is like crafting a roadmap for potential disasters. Begin by prioritizing risks based on the specific hazards your city faces. Is your area prone to flooding or power outages? Tailor your plan to address these risks first. Once you've identified the priorities, schedule regular reviews and updates. As your circumstances change, so should your plan. Maybe you've moved to a new neighborhood, or your family has grown. These changes require adjustments to your preparedness strategy. By keeping your plan dynamic, you ensure it remains relevant and effective.

Embracing a forward-thinking attitude is about looking beyond the immediate and anticipating future challenges. Climate change, for instance, has long-term impacts that can't be ignored. Rising temperatures and increased storm frequency affect urban areas significantly. Understanding these potential changes allows you to adapt your preparedness strategies accordingly. Consider the financial aspect of preparedness, too. Assess your insurance needs and establish a financial safety net. Having a plan for the financial implications of a disaster is as critical as having a plan for the physical ones. Can you put five dollars a week in a jar? It might not be much, but it's a start!

Incorporating these elements into your life transforms preparedness from a daunting task into a natural part of your routine. It's a mindset shift that empowers you to take control of your safety and well-being. As you progress, you'll find that preparedness isn't about living in fear of what might happen. It's about living confidently, knowing you're ready for whatever comes your way.

Activity: Preparedness Goal-Setting Worksheet

Take a moment to write down three specific preparedness goals you want to achieve over the next six months. Consider both tangible tasks, like assembling an emergency kit, and intangible ones, like learning a new skill. For each goal, outline the steps you'll take to accomplish it and set a realistic timeline. Revisit this worksheet regularly to track your progress and make adjustments as needed. This exercise will help you stay focused and motivated on your path to proactive preparedness.

11.2 CULTIVATING A CULTURE OF PREPAREDNESS

IMAGINE your neighborhood coming together for a local disaster drill. The streets, usually filled with the hustle of daily life, now echo with the sounds of shared purpose. Participating in such community preparedness initiatives isn't just about rehearsing emergency procedures—it's about building bonds and fostering collective resilience. By joining neighborhood emergency response teams, like CERT, you're not only gaining valuable skills in fire safety and light search and rescue, but you're also contributing to a network that stands ready to support each other when it matters most. These experiences transform people from mere neighbors into allies, united by a shared commitment to safety and preparedness. They also bring a sense of empowerment, knowing that you're not alone in your efforts to face potential challenges.

Preparedness education is another pillar of fostering a culture of readiness. Getting started is as easy as going to Ready.gov and taking a look around. Sharing knowledge within your social networks can spark interest and motivate others to take action. Consider hosting workshops or seminars in your community center or even your living room. These gatherings can cover a range of topics, from creating emergency kits to understanding local hazards. Social media is a powerful tool in this endeavor. Sharing educational resources online can reach a wider audience, breaking down barriers and making preparedness information accessible to all. A simple post about the importance of having a family emergency plan might inspire a friend to start their own. Every shared story or tip contributes to a broader culture of awareness and readiness, making preparedness a community-wide effort rather than an individual task.

Creating a preparedness-focused environment at home might seem daunting, but small changes can make a big difference. Start by displaying emergency contact information prominently in your living space. A list on the refrigerator or a note by the phone ensures that vital numbers are always within reach. Consider maintaining visible emergency supply stations in your home. Designate a spot in a hallway closet or a corner of the garage for your emergency kit. By making these supplies an integral part of your daily environment, you reinforce the habit of preparedness. It becomes a constant reminder, not just a box tucked away, forgotten until needed. This visibility helps you and your family stay ready and organized, promoting a mindset where preparedness is second nature.

Involving family and friends in preparedness activities strengthens the culture of readiness and makes it a shared experience. Regular family meetings to discuss preparedness plans ensure everyone is on the same page. These gatherings are opportunities to talk about potential scenarios and update plans as needed. Collaborative planning sessions with friends or neighbors can also prove invaluable. Sharing insights and resources can lead to more comprehensive and effective strategies. Imagine sitting around a table, brainstorming evacuation routes, or discussing the best local resources for emergency supplies. These discussions build a sense of community and mutual support, transforming preparedness from an isolated task into a collective effort.

————

Activity: Preparedness Planning Checklist

Start a checklist for your family and friends that includes essential preparedness tasks, like setting up communication plans, identifying safe meeting places, and assembling emergency kits. Share this checklist during your meetings to ensure everyone is aligned and prepared. This simple but effective tool serves as a tangible reminder of what needs to be done, promoting accountability and action.

————

11.3 INTEGRATING PREPAREDNESS INTO DAILY LIFE

IMAGINE STARTING your week with a simple routine—checking your emergency supplies while you sip your morning coffee. It might sound mundane, but this habit ensures you're prepared when the unexpected strikes. Incorporating preparedness into daily routines doesn't require a complete lifestyle overhaul. Instead, it's about weaving small, manageable tasks into the rhythm of your everyday life. Each week, as you tackle household chores, take a moment to inspect your emergency kit. Check expiration dates on food items and ensure flashlights have working batteries. This regular upkeep prevents the last-minute scramble during an actual emergency. By making these checks a part of your routine, you maintain your readiness with minimal effort.

Family outings offer another excellent opportunity to practice preparedness. Next time you head to the park or take a leisurely walk, turn it into an evacuation drill. With your maps in hand, plan routes to nearby safe zones or meeting points. This exercise isn't just practical; it makes preparedness engaging for the whole family. Kids can join in, learning to recognize landmarks and understand the importance of having a plan. After all, practice makes perfect. Familiarizing yourself with these routes means that, in a real crisis, you won't waste precious moments deciding where to go. It becomes second nature, a reflex honed through repetition and familiarity.

Everyday activities also provide chances to build essential skills. Cooking meals with non-perishable ingredients, for example, can be both practical and educational. Challenge yourself to create a delicious dinner using only canned goods and dried foods. This exercise tests your culinary creativity and familiarizes you with the types of foods that store well over time. As you prepare these meals, consider what ingredients you would want in your emergency pantry. Similarly, transform family game night into a first-aid learning session. Practice bandaging techniques or role-play scenarios where basic medical skills might be needed. These activities blend fun and learning, ensuring everyone in the family gains valuable knowledge without the pressure of a formal setting.

Making preparedness a family affair promotes collective readiness and strengthens bonds. Assign age-appropriate roles to each family member, giving everyone a vested interest in the process. Younger children might be responsible for gathering supplies, while older kids can help with organizing and planning. These roles instill a sense of responsibility and teamwork, transforming preparedness into a shared family goal. Consider turning these tasks into educational games or challenges. Who can assemble a mini emergency kit the fastest? Or who can name the most items in the go-bag? These playful activities make learning enjoyable and reinforce the importance of being ready.

Technology can be a powerful ally in keeping preparedness efforts active and up-to-date. Use your smartphone to set reminders for kit updates and maintenance. A monthly alert can prompt you to check your supplies, ensuring everything is in working order. Apps designed for skill development can track your progress and help you learn new emergency skills. Whether it's a first-aid course or a survival skills app, technology offers a wealth of resources at your fingertips. By integrating these digital tools into your preparedness plan, you stay informed and ready, adapting to new challenges as they arise.

Preparedness isn't just a checklist to complete; it's a mindset to cultivate. By embedding these activities into your daily life, you shift from reactive to proactive, transforming preparedness into a seamless part of your routine. It's about being ready for the unexpected while living confidently and securely in the present.

11.4 BUILDING RESILIENCE FOR THE LONG TERM

IN A CITY where change is the only constant, long-term preparedness becomes your ally. It's not just about having a plan for tomorrow but about laying a foundation for years to come. Let's start with food storage. Imagine your pantry not as a temporary reserve but as a sustainable resource. Building a long-term food storage plan isn't about hoarding; it's about smart stocking. Begin by identifying foods with extended shelf lives. Canned beans, rice, and pasta are staples that last. Rotate these items regularly, using them in your everyday meals and replacing them with fresh stock. This practice ensures your supplies stay fresh and useful. As you fill your pantry, you're creating a buffer against disruptions, reducing the stress of sudden shortages.

Your financial safety net is equally crucial. Consider this: a single emergency can cripple finances if you're unprepared. Setting aside a bit of money each month builds a reserve you can rely on when times get tough. Start small. Even a modest amount grows over time. This fund isn't just for disasters—it's a cushion for any unexpected expense. Evaluate your insurance needs, too. Does your policy cover the types of emergencies your city might face? Reviewing your coverage ensures you're protected against financial fallout in a crisis. These steps create a financial foundation that supports you through uncertain times.

Adaptability is your next key asset. Urban life is dynamic, and your preparedness strategies should be, too. As new information emerges or your personal circumstances change, update your plans. Perhaps you've moved to a new apartment or expanded your family. Each change requires a reevaluation of your needs and resources. Adapt your strategies to fit these new contexts. Flexibility ensures your readiness plan remains effective and relevant, no matter what life throws your way. This ability to adapt is what turns a static plan into a living, breathing guide.

Equally important is fostering emotional and psychological resilience. In the face of ongoing challenges, mental strength becomes as vital as physical readiness. Engage in activities that build resilience, like mindfulness or meditation. These practices help you maintain calm and focus, even under pressure. They offer a sanctuary of peace in a bustling urban environment. Sometimes, though, the weight of challenges requires professional support. Don't hesitate to seek help from mental health professionals. Counseling or therapy can provide strategies to manage stress, ensuring you remain balanced and capable.

Continuous learning is the final piece of the puzzle. The world of preparedness is ever-evolving, with new risks and technologies emerging. Stay informed by attending regular training sessions or workshops. These opportunities not only refresh your skills but also introduce you to the latest advancements in disaster readiness. Staying updated means you're not caught off guard by new threats. Engage with resources that challenge and expand your understanding. Whether it's a book, a podcast, or an online course, these tools keep your knowledge sharp and your preparedness strategies robust. This commitment to learning is what transforms preparedness from a task into a lifestyle.

In the grand scheme, building resilience isn't just about individual preparedness. It's about contributing to a larger tapestry of readiness that strengthens entire communities. As you focus on these long-term goals, remember that your efforts ripple outward, encouraging others to do the same. Together, we create a network of support and strength. This network is what ensures urban life remains vibrant and secure, even in the face of uncertainty. In the next chapter, we'll explore practical checklists and quick reference guides, turning the insights and strategies we've discussed into actionable steps for your everyday life.

CHAPTER 12

CHECKLISTS AND QUICK REFERENCE GUIDES

There's a sudden, unexpected knock on your apartment door. You open it to find your neighbor, wide-eyed, informing you of a gas leak in the building. With adrenaline coursing through your veins, you instinctively reach for your go-bag. In that moment, you're grateful for its existence. Your go-bag is more than a backpack filled with essentials; it's your lifeline in emergencies, ready to support you through the uncertainties of urban living. As we dive into this chapter, we'll outline the key components of an effective urban go-bag and plan, ensuring you're prepared for anything the city throws your way.

———

THIS CHAPTER PRESENTS this idea as text, but at the end of the book you will be directed to editable versions of corresponding checklists and quick reference guides.

———

12.2 THE ULTIMATE URBAN GO-BAG CHECKLIST

A sturdy, durable backpack is the cornerstone of your emergency preparedness arsenal. It holds everything you need to sustain yourself, even when the situation turns chaotic. Choose a design that offers comfort and ample storage, with compartments to keep your items organized. This bag will serve as a mobile base, ensuring you carry essential supplies wherever you go. Mobility is crucial in urban settings, and your backpack should be easy to grab and go, whether you're navigating crowded sidewalks or hurrying down stairwells.

Inside, pack a three-day supply of non-perishable food and water. These essentials are your primary sustenance during the initial phase of any emergency. Think energy bars, canned goods, and water pouches that can withstand time and temperature fluctuations. The goal is to have enough to keep you nourished and hydrated while you wait for additional resources or aid. Remember, simplicity is key in a crisis. Choose items that require minimal preparation, offer maximum nutrition, and are lightweight. If you've ever been backpacking or carried a heavy backpack full of schoolbooks, this will make sense!

A multi-tool is your Swiss Army knife of urban survival, offering versatility and utility in a compact form. From opening cans to fixing a loose screw, this tool will become indispensable. Its range of functions can assist you in various scenarios, from making repairs to improvising solutions. Coupled with a first aid kit stocked with basic supplies and prescription medications, you're equipped to handle minor injuries and ailments on the go. This kit is your personal field medic, ready to address cuts, bruises, or any unexpected health hiccups.

Personal items for comfort and security are vital in maintaining morale and health during emergencies. Spare clothing and weather-appropriate gear will keep you comfortable and protect you against the elements. Don't overlook personal hygiene products—travel-sized toiletries keep you fresh and presentable even when circumstances are less than ideal. These items bridge the gap between survival and comfort, offering a semblance of normalcy amid chaos.

You should also include personal identification and important documents, such as copies of your ID, insurance papers, and any critical contacts.

 **Pro Tip:** You should also make sure all of your important documents are saved to a cloud storage location like DropBox, iCloud, or Google Drive. While this isn't the same as having your documents in front of you, it is better than not having them at all.

In today's digital age, tech and communication essentials are paramount. A portable phone charger or power bank ensures your devices remain operational, allowing you to communicate with loved ones and access information. Pair this with a battery-powered radio for updates when digital networks fail. A flashlight with extra batteries is indispensable for navigating darkened environments, while a written list of important locations and phone numbers serves as a backup if digital devices falter. These tools keep you connected, informed, and in control, regardless of technological setbacks.

Financial and resource planning are often overlooked but crucial components of preparedness. Carry cash in small denominations for situations where electronic transactions are unavailable. This ensures you can make purchases, from food to transportation, without relying on digital payment systems. Why small denominations? In an emergency, if the person you are trying to purchase from can't make change, you might go through your large bills faster. Or, in more nefarious cases, if they see that all you have is a ten-dollar bill, then that candy bar will cost you ten dollars. Keep copies of financial and insurance documents within reach, safeguarding your assets and facilitating recovery efforts. These measures provide a safety net, allowing you to manage resources effectively and maintain financial stability amidst disruption.

Activity: Customize Your Go-Bag

Take a moment to start to personalize your go-bag using the ideas above. Consider your unique needs and lifestyle, adding or adjusting items as necessary. Start by making a list, and then start gathering and organizing the items. Once you have it all laid out, review it all to see if you actually need all of it. Think of it like packing for vacation, where you can only bring a carry-on bag. This exercise not only ensures your bag meets your specific requirements but also familiarizes you with its contents, making it second nature to grab and go.

YOUR URBAN GO-BAG is more than just an emergency kit; it's a symbol of readiness, a testament to your proactive approach to urban living. By assembling and maintaining this bag, you empower yourself to face the unpredictable with confidence, knowing you have a reliable foundation to support you through whatever challenges arise.

12.3 QUICK GUIDE TO EMERGENCY COMMUNICATION PLANS

Imagine it's a typical Tuesday evening, and you're unwinding after a long day when, without warning, the power goes out. You peer out your window and see that the entire block is dark. Your first instinct is to reach for your phone, but then you remember how crucial communication becomes in times like this. Establishing reliable communication channels is a cornerstone of urban preparedness. One of the simplest yet most effective strategies is designating a family contact person who lives outside the affected area. This person becomes the central point for updates and coordination. By funneling information through a single, reliable source, you minimize confusion and ensure consistent communication. This setup allows family members to check in with one person, who then relays information to everyone else, keeping the lines open and reducing the risk of misinformation.

Setting up a group messaging app specifically for emergencies is another practical step. These apps allow you to create a dedicated space where family and friends can exchange updates and coordinate plans. Whether it's WhatsApp, Signal, or another app of your choice, the key is ease of use and reliability. These platforms offer real-time communication, and many work even when the phone networks are congested. You can share your location, send voice notes, and even attach photos if needed. This digital gathering place ensures everyone is on the same page, from the initial alert to the all-clear signal. It's about creating a virtual meeting room where everyone can connect, share, and support each other through the crisis.

A communication tree further enhances the efficiency of your communication plan. This involves identifying key contact points within your family and assigning roles for information relay. Think of it as a flowchart where information follows a clear path. For example, you might be responsible for updating your immediate family, while your sibling communicates with extended relatives. This organized approach ensures that messages reach everyone without delay or distortion. In a world where misinformation spreads as quickly as wildfire, having a structured plan to pass along accurate information is invaluable. It curtails the rumor mill and keeps everyone informed with factual and timely updates.

Emergencies can disrupt primary communication methods, so having backup options is crucial. Pre-arranged meeting points offer a physical space for family members to regroup if phone lines are down. These locations should be familiar, easily accessible, and safe. Maybe it's the park a few blocks away or a nearby café. Wherever you choose, make sure everyone knows the spot and can get there without hassle. Walkie-talkies or ham radios also provide reliable alternatives. These devices operate independently of cell networks, offering a direct line of communication that's both secure and dependable. They're especially useful in urban environments, where tall buildings can interfere with cell signals.

Regular communication drills ensure your plan is not just theoretical but practical and effective. Conduct bi-annual family communication drills to practice your setup. During these drills, simulate different scenarios, like a power outage or a natural disaster, and test how well your communication channels hold up. This practice helps identify weak spots in your plan and gives everyone a chance to familiarize themselves with their roles. It's like a fire drill but for your communication strategy, reinforcing the importance of preparedness and ensuring everyone knows what to do when it counts. Additionally, periodically test your emergency contact numbers to verify they are up-to-date and functional. This step might seem minor, but it's crucial. Outdated or incorrect numbers can thwart even the best-laid plans.

Activity: Create Your Communication Tree

Take a moment now to sketch out your communication tree. Identify who will communicate with whom and establish clear lines of responsibility. This exercise solidifies your plan and provides a visual reference to keep everyone organized and informed. Keep this tree in a place where it's easily accessible, ensuring that in the midst of chaos, your communication plan remains a beacon of clarity and calm.

12.4 CHECKLIST FOR FAMILY AND PET SAFETY

IT'S 3 A.M., and the sudden blare of a smoke alarm wakes you in the dead of night. You feel a rush of urgency as your mind races through the mental checklist you've prepared for just such an emergency. This scenario underscores the vital importance of having a tailored emergency plan for each family member. Begin by considering the unique layout of your home. Every residence has its quirks, and your safety drills should reflect these specifics. Practice regularly with your family so everyone knows the best routes to safety. Designate safe rooms that provide protection and security in case evacuation isn't immediately possible. These rooms should be easily accessible and stocked with basic supplies. Fire escape plans are equally crucial. Identify every possible exit and ensure everyone knows how to reach them quickly. Practicing these plans reduces panic in real situations, turning potential chaos into calm, coordinated action.

Pets are family, too, and their safety requires special consideration. Equip your furry friends with identification tags and microchips, ensuring they're traceable if they get lost. In an emergency, stress levels are high, and pets can act unpredictably. A microchip is a simple yet effective way to increase the chances of a happy reunion should you become separated. During an evacuation, having a pet carrier and leash at the ready is non-negotiable. These tools help keep your pets secure and under control, minimizing the risk of them running off in fear. Furthermore, stockpile a supply of pet food and water, just as you would for your human family members. Pets have dietary needs just like us, and maintaining their routine as much as possible during a crisis provides comfort and stability.

When it comes to family members with special needs, a one-size-fits-all approach simply won't do. Tailor your emergency plan to address specific requirements, whether they involve medication, equipment, or mobility aids. Compile a detailed list of all necessary medications and medical equipment, and ensure these items are easy to grab quickly. Being prepared means having more than just the right prescriptions on hand; it involves knowing where everything is and having it accessible. Communication aids are also vital for those who require them. Whether it's a speech-generating device or a simple notepad, these tools ensure everyone can communicate effectively, even under stress.

Let's not forget about the mental and emotional well-being of your family. In the midst of an emergency, fear, and stress can take a significant toll. Prepare comfort items for children, like a favorite stuffed animal or blanket, to help soothe and reassure them. These small tokens can have a big impact, providing a sense of normalcy and security. Access to mental health support lines is also crucial. Knowing there are professionals available to talk to can alleviate anxiety and provide much-needed guidance. Encourage open communication within your family about feelings and fears. Discussing emotions isn't just about addressing immediate needs; it's about fostering resilience and understanding, helping everyone cope better with the challenges they face.

———

Activity: Schedule Time for the Family Plan

Time with your family is probably already limited and heavily planned out. Most of us operate at home the same way we do at work; if it isn't on the calendar, it most likely won't happen. Take a look at the calendar and plan a time when everyone is free to sit down at the table to talk about preparedness. Planning this out for a time in the future and putting it on the calendar gives everyone time to "prepare" for the meeting.

———

12.5 QUICK REFERENCE FOR LOCAL EMERGENCY CONTACTS

IT'S LATE EVENING, and suddenly, you find yourself standing on the sidewalk looking up at smoke rising from your apartment building. In such moments, having a comprehensive and up-to-date list of emergency contacts becomes invaluable. This isn't just about jotting down a few numbers; it's about creating a robust network of support that's ready when you need it most. We aren't talking about how to reach the fire or police department; in the U.S., 9-1-1 is always your go-to for that. However, if you live in another country or plan to visit another country, it is a great idea to research how to get help in an emergency in advance. Start with the basics. Which contacts have you made arrangements with in advance to be able to stay with in the event you're displaced from your home? Yes, eventually, you should call your parents, but if they don't live in the city with you, it's better to start with your immediate needs and then handle updates. Also, in cases of displaced residents, the fire department typically works with the local American Red Cross to help find places for residents. For smaller incidents, this can be hotel rooms, but in cases where an entire apartment building must be rehoused, this typically means a shelter. As you develop your preparedness plan, you will be more comfortable and resilient if you have arranged your own shelter.

Next, extend this list to include a prioritized list of notifications you should make. Do you need to call work before you call your parents? Don't just assume you will know whom to call and when. Brainstorm how different situations will impact your life, and create a notification list for each situation. If you try to figure this out at the moment, it will only add to your stress and may lead to delaying the help you could get.

Don't stop there. Your community is rich with resources designed to support residents in times of need. Contact information for nearby hospitals and clinics should be at your fingertips. In an emergency, quick access to medical assistance is paramount, and knowing where to go can save precious time. Moreover, familiarize yourself with local shelters and food banks. These organizations provide essential services during crises, offering shelter, meals, and other support to those in need. Having their details ready means you won't waste time searching for help when every second counts.

Community centers and volunteer organizations are often the unsung heroes during emergencies. These groups mobilize quickly to offer assistance, coordinate resources, and provide a sense of community in challenging times. Whether it's a place to charge your phone or a warm meal, knowing where these centers are located and how to reach them keeps you connected to the support network around you. Consider these contacts as part of your broader emergency plan, ensuring you have multiple avenues of assistance should the need arise.

Maintaining an effective emergency contact list requires regular updates. Make it a habit to review and revise your list quarterly.

People move, numbers change, and new resources become available. By keeping your list current, you ensure it remains a reliable tool during emergencies. Consider storing digital copies of your contact list on cloud services. This way, you can access the information from any device, even if your primary phone is unavailable. This digital backup adds an extra layer of security, ensuring that your emergency contacts are never out of reach.

Your emergency contact list is more than just names and numbers; it's a lifeline, connecting you to the support and resources necessary to navigate crises effectively. It empowers you to act swiftly and confidently when faced with the unexpected. By compiling and maintaining this list, you lay the groundwork for a resilient response, ensuring that help is always within reach.

CONCLUSION

As you close this book, let's take a moment to reflect on the importance of urban preparedness. Living in a city offers many conveniences and opportunities, but it also presents unique challenges when disaster strikes. The density, infrastructure, and pace of urban life require a different approach to readiness. Being prepared isn't about fear; it's about empowerment. It's about ensuring that you and your loved ones are safe and secure no matter what happens.

Throughout this book, we've explored a wide range of topics to help you navigate the complexities of urban preparedness. You've learned how to assess the risks specific to your city, such as floods, power outages, and civil unrest. We've dived into the essential tools and technologies that keep you informed and connected during emergencies. You now know how to build an affordable emergency kit and utilize space efficiently in your home. We've also discussed the value of community connections and the importance of fostering resilience, both individually and collectively.

The key takeaways from these discussions are actionable insights that you can implement today. Start by understanding the specific risks in your area and tailor your preparedness plans accordingly. Utilize technology to stay informed and connected. Build your emergency kit piece by piece, focusing on essentials that fit your budget. Engage with your community to build a support network that extends beyond your immediate household.

But this is just the beginning. Preparedness is not a one-time task; it's a lifestyle choice. It empowers you to face uncertainty with confidence. By adopting a forward-thinking approach, you transform potential challenges into opportunities for growth and resilience. Think of preparedness as an investment in your future, one that pays dividends in peace of mind and security.

Here's what I urge you to do next: take immediate steps toward implementing the strategies we've discussed. Start small. Perhaps today, you can create a family communication plan or download a local emergency alert app. Tomorrow, you might inventory your supplies or attend a community meeting to connect with neighbors. Each action, no matter how minor, contributes to your overall readiness.

Let me share a personal message. After 25 years in emergency management, I've witnessed the profound impact that even a small amount of preparedness can have. I've seen communities come together in remarkable ways, and I've seen individuals rise to challenges they never imagined facing. My passion for this work stems from a deep commitment to helping urban residents like you become more resilient. Your safety and well-being are what drive me to share my knowledge and experiences.

There are numerous resources available to help you continue your journey. Websites like Ready.gov offer a wealth of information tailored to your needs. Local emergency management offices often provide workshops and materials specific to your area. Books and online courses can further expand your knowledge and skills. Stay connected with community organizations that focus on preparedness and resilience. They are invaluable allies in your quest for readiness.

Remember, you're not alone in this journey. The steps you take today will **PREPARE** you and strengthen your community. Together, we can build a future where urban life thrives, even in the face of adversity. Embrace the power of preparedness, and let it guide you toward a safer, more secure tomorrow.

RESOURCES

Download the Checklists and Quick Reference Guides

To accompany this book, I've created a series of Checklists and Quick Reference Guides that you can download anytime. These are freely available at the link below. Additionally, these resources will be updated over time, so feel free to check back often for the latest version.

TLCTRNG.com/prepare

PLEASE GIVE YOUR REVIEW

Keeping Preparedness Alive

Now that you've got the tools and knowledge to feel ready for the unexpected, it's time to share what you've learned and help others discover the same sense of confidence and security.

By leaving your honest opinion of *PREPARE* on Amazon, you'll guide others who are looking for practical, no-nonsense advice on disaster preparedness. Your review can show fellow readers that being ready doesn't have to be overwhelming—it can fit right into everyday life.

We build preparedness together. The message grows stronger when we pass on our knowledge, and by sharing your thoughts, you help keep this important conversation alive.

Thank you for participating in this mission. Together, we can empower more people to take simple steps toward resilience.

Click here to leave your review on Amazon

Or use the QR Code

Be Prepared,

Travis L. Cryan

———

COMING SOON
Two additional books in the series!
PREPARE: Small Towns and Suburbs
AND
SURVIVE: When the Worst Happens

While PREPARE focused on the preparedness for those living in the urban environment, PREPARE: Small Towns and Suburbs will be more appropriate for those outside the urban jungles.

After that, SURVIVE will focus on how to put the knowledge, skills, and resources you gathered in either PREPARE book into practice when the next disaster happens.

Email Prepare@TLCTRNG.com for early access

REFERENCES

1. American Red Cross. (n.d.). **Make a first aid kit: Supplies & contents.** Retrieved December 6, 2024, from https://www.redcross.org/get-help/how-to-prepare-for-emergencies/anatomy-of-a-first-aid-kit.html

2. American Red Cross. (n.d.). **Pet disaster preparedness & recovery.** Retrieved December 6, 2024, from https://www.redcross.org/get-help/how-to-prepare-for-emergencies/pet-disaster-preparedness.html

3. BePrepared.com. (n.d.). **Lessons learned, volume 1: Natalie survived the Northeast blackout of 2003.** Retrieved December 6, 2024, from https://www.beprepared.com/blogs/articles/lessons-learned-volume-1-natalie-survived-the-northeast-blackout-of-2003

4. Bug Out Bag Builder. (n.d.). **Bug out bag list & essentials.** Retrieved December 6, 2024, from https://www.bugoutbagbuilder.com/learning-tutorials/bug-out-bag

5. CNET. (2024). **Best tested portable power stations in 2024.** Retrieved December 6, 2024, from https://www.cnet.com/home/energy-and-utilities/best-portable-power-stations/

6. FEMA. (n.d.). **Building code lessons from the 1994 Northridge earthquake.** Retrieved December 6, 2024, from https://www.fema.gov/case-study/building-code-lessons-1994-northridge-earthquake

7. FEMA. (n.d.). **Community Emergency Response Team (CERT).** Retrieved December 6, 2024, from https://www.fema.gov/emergency-managers/individuals-communities/preparedness-activities-webinars/community-emergency-response-team

8. Going Zero Waste. (n.d.). **How to build an eco-friendly emergency kit.** Retrieved December 6, 2024, from https://www.goingzerowaste.com/blog/how-to-build-an-eco-friendly-emergency-kit/

9. Harris County Flood Control District. (n.d.). **Hurricane Harvey: Harris County's flooding history.** Retrieved December 6, 2024, from https://www.hcfcd.org/About/Harris-Countys-Flooding-History/Hurricane-Harvey

10. Homes & Gardens. (n.d.). **7 ways to use vertical storage to save space.** Retrieved December 6, 2024, from https://www.homesandgardens.com/solved/space-saving-ways-to-use-vertical-storage

11. Homestead How-To. (n.d.). **14 everyday items preppers should reuse instead of tossing.** Retrieved December 6, 2024, from https://homesteadhow-to.com/everyday-items-every-prepper-should-reuse-instead-of-tossing/

12. Insight Psychology Group. (n.d.). **Mindfulness exercises for the stressful city life.** Retrieved December 6, 2024, from https://www.insightpsychologygroup.com/blog/mindfulness-exercises-stressful-city-life?format=amp

13. Jotform. (n.d.). **Emergency contact list - Table templates.** Retrieved December

6, 2024, from https://www.jotform.com/table-templates/emergency-contact-list

14. L-Squared. (n.d.). **Digital communication: Planning for emergency notification situations.** Retrieved December 6, 2024, from https://lsquared.com/blog-list/digital-communication-planning-for-emergency-notification-situations

15. Massachusetts Nurses Association. (2007, March 15). **Promoting emotional resilience for disaster and emergency incidents.** Retrieved December 6, 2024, from https://www.massnurses.org/2007/03/15/promoting-emotional-resilience-for-disaster-and-emergency-incidents/

16. New York Times. (2020, June 6). **How to start a neighborhood association.** Retrieved December 6, 2024, from https://www.nytimes.com/2020/06/06/smarter-living/how-to-start-a-neighborhood-association.html

17. NIST Global. (2023). **Top 8 tips for conducting an effective emergency drill.** Retrieved December 6, 2024, from https://nistglobal.com/blog/2023/08/top-8-tips-for-conducting-an-effective-emergency-drill/

18. Office of the Assistant Secretary for Preparedness and Response. (n.d.). **Social media in emergency response.**Retrieved December 6, 2024, from https://asprtracie.hhs.gov/technical-resources/73/social-media-in-emncy-response/77

19. Outdoor Gear Lab. (2024). **The best 6 portable solar chargers of 2024: Tested and reviewed.** Retrieved December 6, 2024, from https://www.outdoorgearlab.com/topics/camping-and-hiking/best-portable-solar-charger

20. Ready.gov. (n.d.). **Build a kit.** Retrieved December 6, 2024, from https://www.ready.gov/kit

21. Ready.gov. (n.d.). **Evacuation.** Retrieved December 6, 2024, from https://www.ready.gov/evacuation

22. Ready.gov. (n.d.). **Preparedness community home.** Retrieved December 6, 2024, from https://community.fema.gov/PreparednessCommunity/s/?language=en_US

23. Reddit. (n.d.). **Stores to get supplies.** Retrieved December 6, 2024, from https://www.reddit.com/r/Survival/comments/10vn6bh/stores_to_get_supplies/

24. Resource Furniture. (n.d.). **Seven sneaky storage solutions for small spaces.** Retrieved December 6, 2024, from https://resourcefurniture.com/blogs/blog/seven-sneaky-storage-solutions-for-small-spaces

25. RTI International. (n.d.). **3 key ways to improve disaster risk reduction in cities.** Retrieved December 6, 2024, from https://www.rti.org/insights/ways-to-improve-disaster-risk-reduction-in-cities

26. Rural Sprout. (n.d.). **How to set up a rainwater collection system & 8 DIY ideas.** Retrieved December 6, 2024, from https://www.ruralsprout.com/rainwater-collection/

27. SAMHSA. (n.d.). **Disaster responder stress management.** Retrieved December 6, 2024, from https://www.samhsa.gov/dtac/disaster-response-template-toolkit/disaster-responder-stress-management

28. ScienceDirect. (2022). **Crisis communication in a blackout scenario.** *International Journal of Disaster Risk Reduction, 77.* Retrieved December 6, 2024, from https://www.sciencedirect.com/science/article/pii/S2212420922000759

29. SmartSheet. (n.d.). **Free crisis communication plan templates.** Retrieved December 6, 2024, from https://www.smartsheet.com/content/crisis-communication-templates

30. Stanford University. (n.d.). **Geolocation-based evacuation routes.** Retrieved December 6, 2024, from https://bigearthhacks.stanford.edu/geolocation-based-evacuation-routes

31. Sutton, J., Olson, M. K., & Waugh, N. A. (2024). **The warning lexicon: A multiphased study to identify, design, and develop content for warning messages.** *Natural Hazards Review, 25*(1). https://doi.org/10.1061/nhrefo.nheng-1900

32. Terra Frma. (n.d.). **Expert tips for overcoming your fear of natural disasters.** Retrieved December 6, 2024, from https://terrafrma.com/blogs/news/overcoming-your-fear-of-natural-disasters

33. The Community Foundation. (n.d.). **Mutual aid groups: Preparing for tomorrow's crises by investing in today's problem solvers.** Retrieved December 6, 2024, from https://www.thecommunityfoundation.org/news/mutual-aid-groups-preparing-for-tomorrows-crises-by-investing-in-todays-problem-solvers

34. The Penny Hoarder. (n.d.). **8 tips to build an emergency kit on a budget.** Retrieved December 6, 2024, from https://www.thepennyhoarder.com/save-money/build-an-emergency-kit-on-a-budget/

35. The Provident Prepper. (n.d.). **Safe indoor emergency cooking solutions.** Retrieved December 6, 2024, from https://theprovidentprepper.org/safe-indoor-emergency-cooking-solutions/

36. The Spruce. (n.d.). **15 space-saving furniture solutions for small spaces.** Retrieved December 6, 2024, from https://www.thespruce.com/transforming-furniture-for-small-spaces-4058276

37. The Spruce. (n.d.). **The 9 best under-bed storage of 2024, tested and reviewed.** Retrieved December 6, 2024, from https://www.thespruce.com/best-under-bed-storage-organizers-4154707

38. U.S. Environmental Protection Agency. (n.d.). **Climate change impacts on the built environment.** Retrieved December 6, 2024, from https://www.epa.gov/climateimpacts/climate-change-impacts-built-environment

39. UNDP. (n.d.). **Community risk assessment: Facilitators' guidebook.** Retrieved December 6, 2024, from https://www.adaptation-undp.org/resources/training-tools/community-risk-assessment-facilitators-guidebook

40. UNDP. (n.d.). **Innovation in disaster management: Leveraging technology to save more lives.** Retrieved December 6, 2024, from https://www.undp.org/policy-centre/istanbul/publications/innovation-disaster-management-leveraging-technology-save-more-lives

41. Walden University. (n.d.). **Why emergency preparedness matters.** Retrieved December 6, 2024, from https://www.waldenu.edu/online-masters-

programs/ms-in-criminal-justice/resource/why-emergency-preparedness-matters

42. Wang, S., & Shen, Y. (2021). **Rethinking disaster resilience in high-density cities.** *Sustainable Cities and Society, 74.*Retrieved December 6, 2024, from https://www.sciencedirect.com/science/article/abs/pii/S2210670721001402

43. Wikipedia. (n.d.). **2019–2020 Hong Kong protests.** Retrieved December 6, 2024, from https://en.wikipedia.org/wiki/2019%E2%80%932020_Hong_Kong_protests

44. Wired. (n.d.). **Which safety app should you trust for personal protection?** Retrieved December 6, 2024, from https://www.wired.com/gallery/which-personal-safety-app-is-best-for-me/

45. RTI International. (n.d.). **3 key ways to improve disaster risk reduction in cities.** Retrieved December 6, 2024, from https://www.rti.org/insights/ways-to-improve-disaster-risk-reduction-in-cities

46. SmartSheet. (n.d.). **Free crisis communication plan templates.** Retrieved December 6, 2024, from https://www.smartsheet.com/content/crisis-communication-templates